RED FOLEY

A longtime baseball writer who has worked thirty-five years for the New York *Daily News*, Red Foley presently serves as an Official Scorer in New York for both the American and National Leagues. A scorer for eighteen seasons, he has worked both the All Star Game and World Series.

In addition, he conducts a Sunday feature in the New York *Daily News* called "Ask Red" in which Foley answers fans' baseball questions. He is the Assistant Secretary of the Baseball Writers' Association of America, with which he has been affiliated since 1962. Foley has also contributed to several baseball books and magazines and is considered by many to be the most knowledgeable baseball historian in the New York area.

Red attends every Yankees and Mets game played in New York.

In order to publish this book for the start of the 1989 baseball season it was necessary to prepare it during the course of the 1988 baseball season. Trades and changes in statistics and other baseball data might have occurred since completion of the manuscript, and some of this data might not be included in the book.

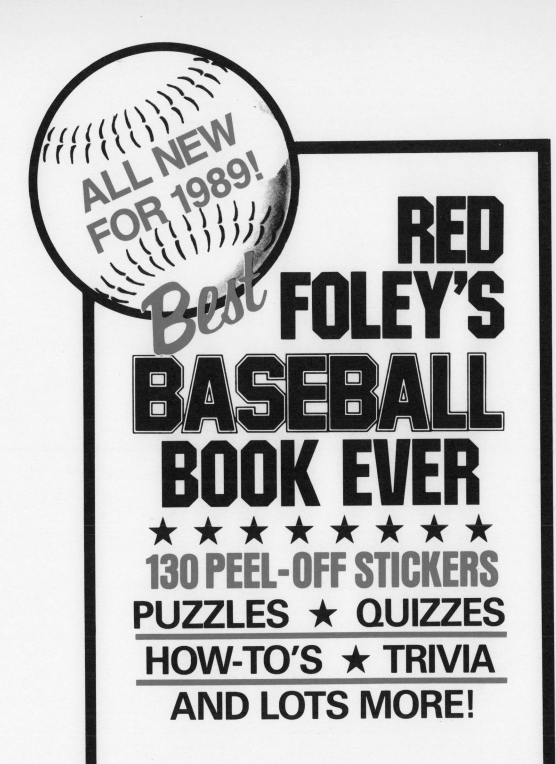

ALL NEW FOR 1989!

Best

RED FOLEY'S BASEBALL BOOK EVER

★ ★ ★ ★ ★ ★ ★ ★ ★ ★ ★

130 PEEL-OFF STICKERS

PUZZLES ★ QUIZZES

HOW-TO'S ★ TRIVIA

AND LOTS MORE!

Little Simon
Published by Simon & Schuster, Inc., New York

Illustrated by Jane Lieman

To Brendan Foley
Still My All-Time ''All Star''

ACKNOWLEDGMENTS

TEN HALL OF FAMERS — WHO AM I? Photos Courtesy of The National Baseball
Hall of Fame and Museum, Inc.
THE HALL OF FAME — Babe Ruth Carving, The Hall of Fame Gallery, Tobacco
and Gum Card Display — Photos courtesy of The National Baseball Hall of Fame
and Museum, Inc.
FUTURE HALL OF FAMERS — RED'S PICK — Baseball cards courtesy of The
Topps Co.
ROOKIES NOT BOTHERED BY THE SOPHOMORE JINX — Baseball cards
courtesy of The Topps Co.

STICKER AND COVER PHOTOS:
Atlanta, Baltimore, Boston, California (Joyner, Howell), Chicago Cubs, Chicago
White Sox, Cincinnati, Cleveland, Detroit, Houston, Kansas City, Los Angeles,
Montreal, New York Mets, New York Yankees, Oakland, Philadelphia, Pittsburgh,
San Francisco, St. Louis, Texas, and Toronto players — *photographs by TOM DIPACE*
Milwaukee players — courtesy of the Milwaukee Brewers
Minnesota players — photographs by Steve Babineau
San Diego players — courtesy of the San Diego Padres
Seattle players — courtesy of the Seattle Mariners
Boston player (Lee Smith) — courtesy of the Boston Red Sox
California players (Johnny Ray, Chili Davis) — courtesy of the California Angels
Pittsburgh player (Brian Fisher) — courtesy of the Pittsburgh Pirates

CONTENTS

TRIVIA QUIZ

CHICAGO
CUBS

Answers on page 94
Place stickers on opposite page

1. A product of Mississippi State, this Hawaiian-born outfielder gave the Cubs some hitting from the left side of the plate last year. A .306 average and a league-leading 95 RBIs made him the Eastern League's MVP at Pittsfield in 1986.

2. The National League's MVP in 1987, this former Expos outfielder became a Cub via free agency. His league-leading 49 homers and 137 RBIs in 1987 easily justified the Cubs' desire to sign him.

3. This righthander won just six games for the Cubs in 1987. But last year, as a sophomore, he proved his ability when he placed himself among the NL's top pitchers in wins, innings pitched and ERA.

4. A member of the Cubs for the past eight seasons, this righthand-hitting catcher has given them power at the plate and stability behind it.

5. The No. 1 player drafted in June 1982, this strong-armed infielder really blossomed last season. He not only made the All Star team, but displayed a potent bat and became one of the NL's top fielders.

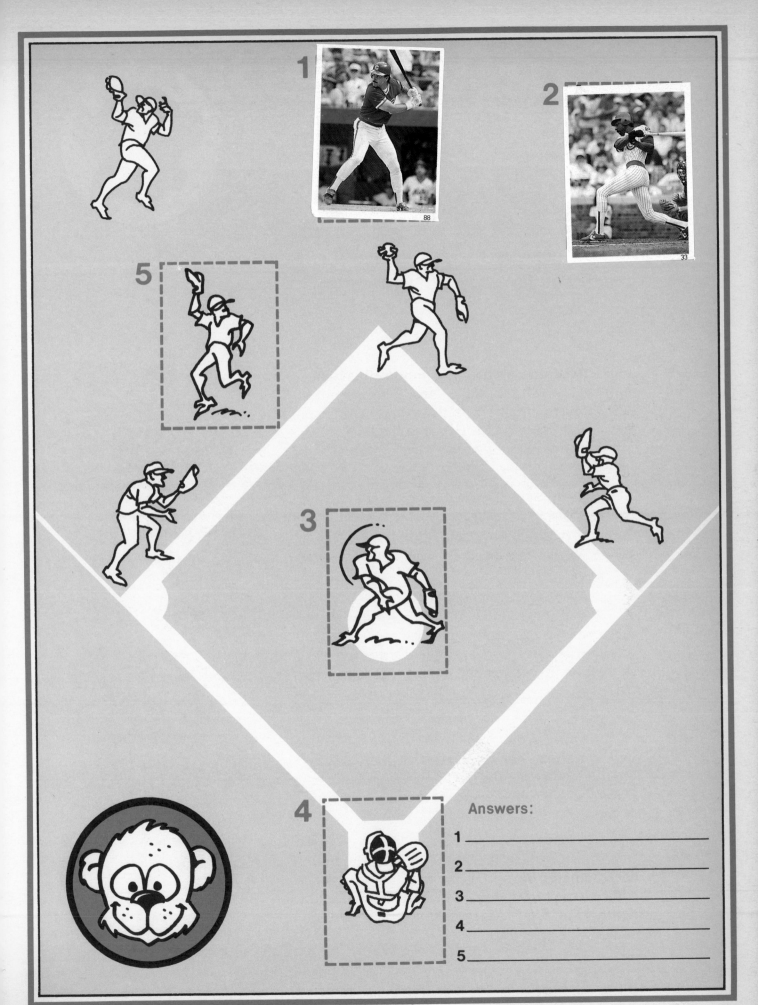

Answers:

1 _____
2 _____
3 _____
4 _____
5 _____

TRIVIA QUIZ

MONTREAL
EXPOS

Answers on page 94
Place stickers on opposite page

1. A home-run hitter in the minors, this right-handed swinger hit .300 the past two years and has supplied his club with the expected longball. He also represented the Expos in the 1988 All Star game.

2. Four times the National League's stolen-base leader, this switchhitting outfielder is a career .300 batter. In addition he's also hitting .300 for his seven appearances in the All Star game.

3. One of those who homered in his first major league at bat, this righthanded hitter almost annually leads National League third basemen in putouts. In 1987 he had a career high 128 runs batted in.

4. Considered the righthanded "stopper" in the Expos' bullpen, he was formerly property of the Pirates and Yankees before Montreal got him in December 1983. In 1985 he set the NL mark for appearances by a rookie with 78.

5. A onetime Met, this righthanded hitter has been bothered by injuries the past two seasons. In addition to playing third and short, he switched to rightfield for the Expos in 1988.

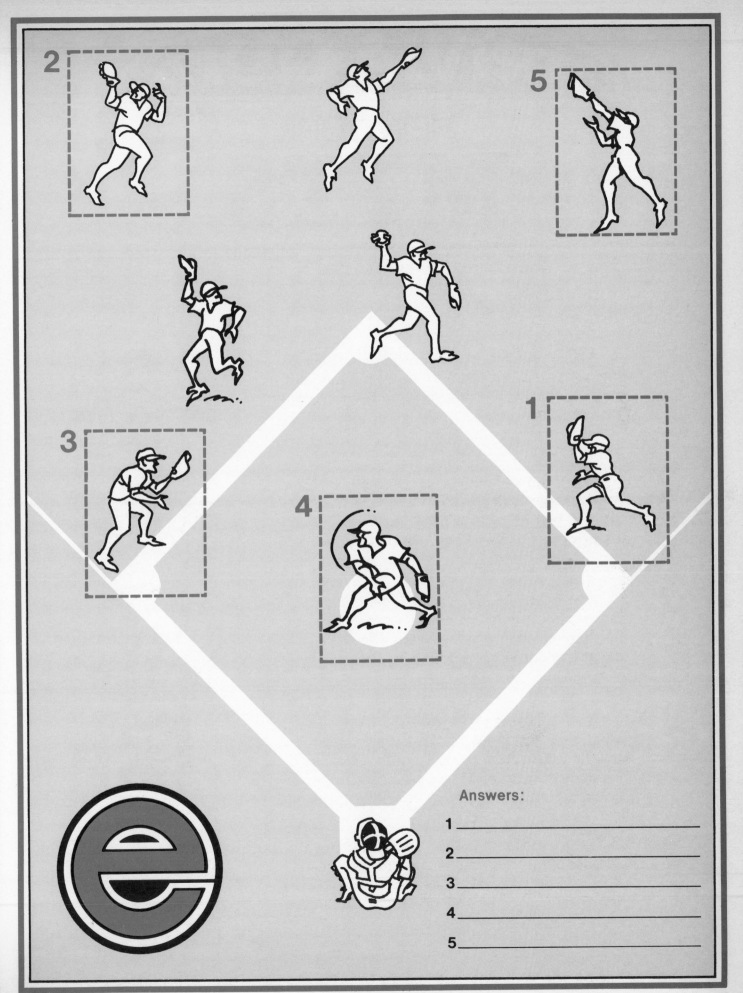

Answers:

1 _____

2 _____

3 _____

4 _____

5 _____

TRIVIA QUIZ

NEW YORK
METS

Answers on page 94
Place stickers on opposite page

1. One of the game's most publicized pitchers, this righthander has been an All Star in four of his five seasons. His 276 strikeouts in 1984 is a record for a rookie pitcher.

2. A leg injury at mid-season idled this veteran for more than a month of the 1988 season and his absence hurt his ballclub. A stellar defensive performer, he's one of baseball's timeliest hitters.

3. Obtained from Kansas City in March 1987, a finger injury bothered him that season. However, he did rebound in 1988 to become a big winner on the staff and was selected for the All Star team.

4. This veteran of 10 All Star games came from Montreal in December 1984. A batting slump slowed him down in much of the 1988 season but in his 15 years he has established many defensive records.

5. Mets' fans consider him "Mr. Everything" because of his talent and longball abilities. The Rookie of the Year in 1983, he has appeared in five straight All Star games and is annually among the Mets leaders in stolen bases.

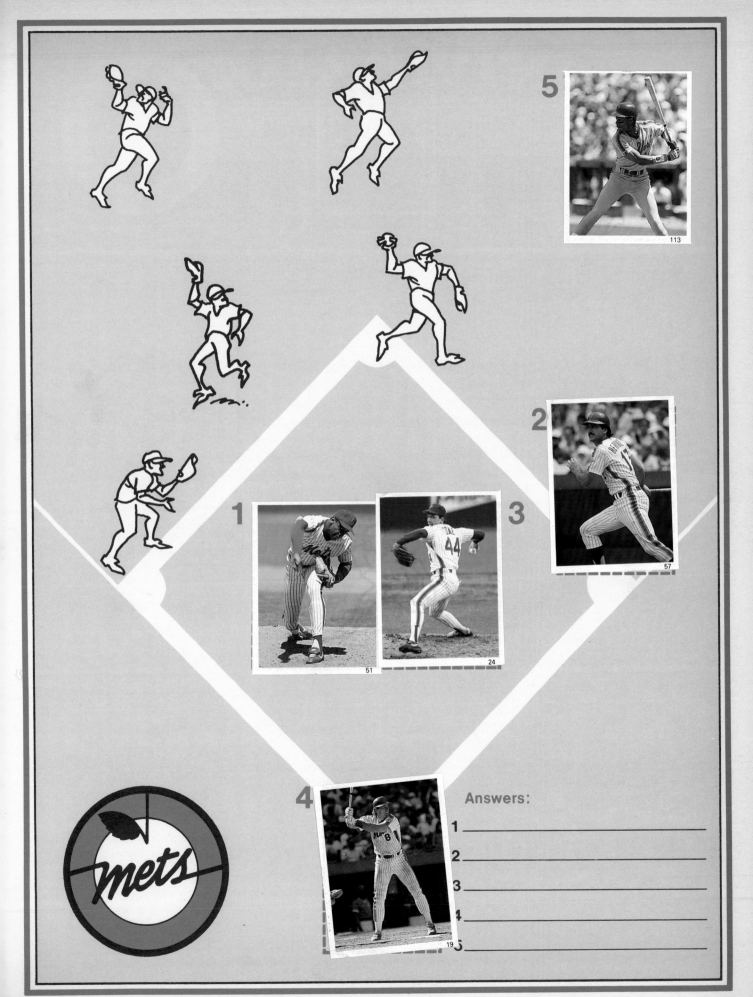

5

2

3

1

4

113

57

51

24

19

mets

Answers:

1 _____

2 _____

3 _____

4 _____

5 _____

TRIVIA QUIZ

PHILADELPHIA
PHILLIES

Answers on page 94
Place stickers on opposite page

1. Leading all active players in lifetime home runs, this power-hitting infielder still contributes defensively. The NL home-run titlist eight times, he has also been its MVP on three occasions.

2. Always among the league leaders in three-base hits, he has stolen more than 230 bases in six major league seasons. In 1987 this busy infielder hit a career high 28 homers and had 100 RBIs.

3. Acquired from Atlanta prior to the 1986 season, this lefthand-hitting outfielder gives the Phillies speed both on base and in the field. He was the Braves' second-round draft pick in January 1979.

4. Injuries limited him in 1988, but in previous years this first baseman-outfielder gave the Phillies consistent performances at the plate and on the bases. In December 1982, Philadelphia dealt five players to get him from Cleveland.

5. This righthand-hitting outfielder, whom the Phillies signed as a free agent in October 1981, has the potential to hit home runs and drive runners in. His brother is a running back for the NFL Patriots.

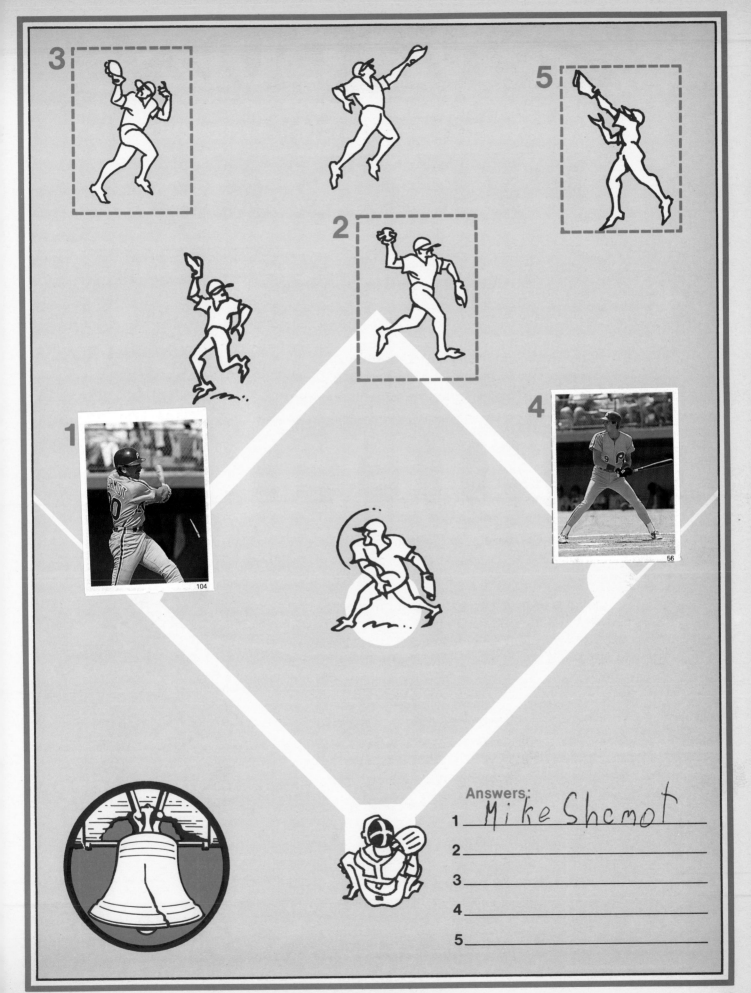

3

5

2

4

104

56

Answers:

1 _Mike Shemot_

2 _____

3 _____

4 _____

5 _____

TRIVIA QUIZ

PITTSBURGH
PIRATES

Answers on page 94
Place stickers on opposite page

1. Home runs and runs batted in from this switchhitter were a prime reason for the Pirates' rise in 1988. Obtained from the White Sox in July 1986, this infielder hit .300 in 1987 and had 77 RBIs.

2. The National League's Gold Glove catcher in 1987, this lefthanded hitter has provided the Pirates with some timely hitting. Originally with St. Louis, he was dealt to Pittsburgh just prior to the 1987 season.

3. Last year was his second as a member of the Pirates, having been dealt from the Yankees in November 1986. The righthander won 11 games in 1987 and has been a regular in the Bucs' mound rotation since.

4. Signed as a free agent in 1982, this acrobatic second baseman advanced to the Pirates during the 1987 season. Since then he has given them some badly needed defense.

5. Following in his father's footsteps, this outfielder has both power and speed. Unlike his daddy, however, he bats and throws lefthanded. But like his famed poppa, he hits homers, drives in runners and, when healthy, steals bases.

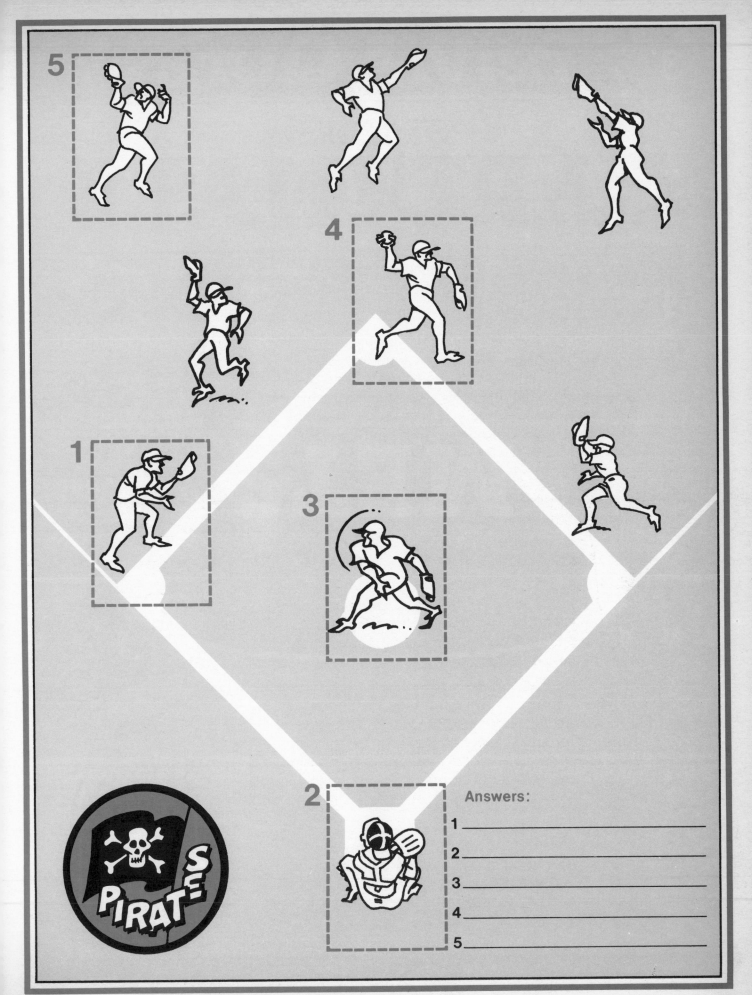

Answers:

1 _____

2 _____

3 _____

4 _____

5 _____

TRIVIA QUIZ

ST. LOUIS
CARDINALS

Answers on page 94
Place stickers on opposite page

1. Obtained from the Twins during the 1988 season, this righthanded hitter supplied the power the Cardinals wanted in their lineup. During his six seasons in Minnesota he was among the club's home-run and RBI leaders.

2. A member of the National League All Star team the past eight years, this switchhitting shortstop holds a bag of fielding records for his defensive play. He's also among the club's leaders in stolen bases.

3. This switchhitting infielder was promoted from the minors last season and demonstrated an ability to fit into the Cardinals' plans. Not a powerhitter, he can play second and can run the bases.

4. Traded to the Dodgers in August, 1988, he is one of the game's top lefthanded pitchers, having won 21 for St. Louis in 1985. He pitched for Boston and Pittsburgh prior to becoming a Cardinal in 1985.

5. A strikeout pitcher, this Dominican righthander joined St. Louis last year. He'd previously worked for the Pirates and White Sox, and despite not having fancy records still remains a mound prospect.

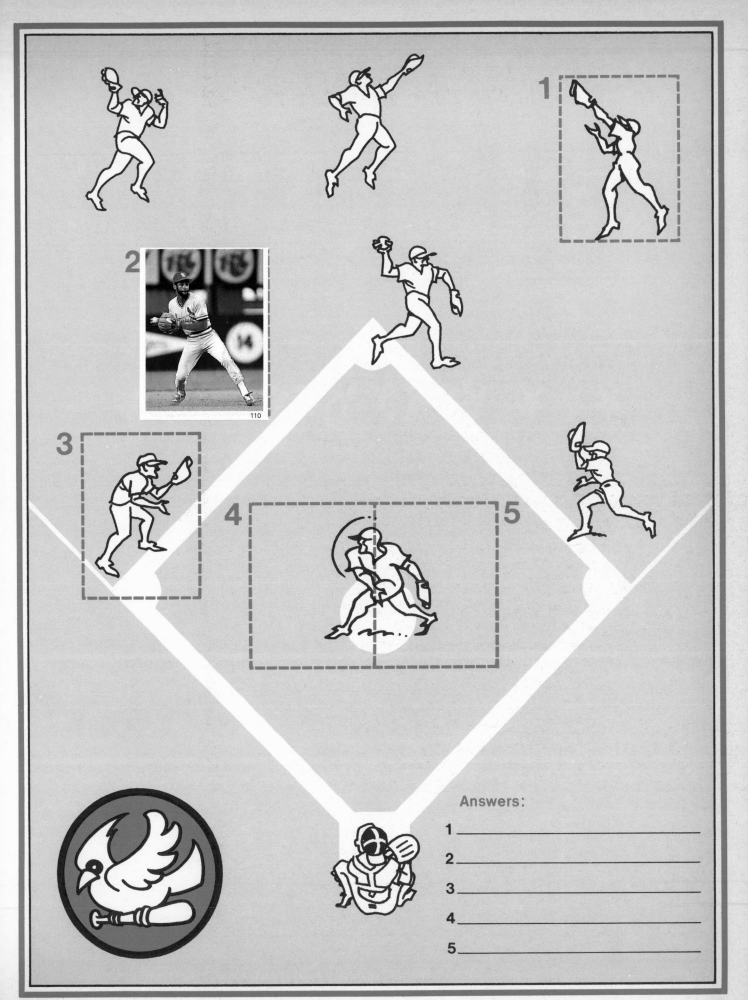

Answers:

1 _____

2 _____

3 _____

4 _____

5 _____

THE HALL OF FAME

This year marks the 50th anniversary of the formal opening of the Hall of Fame and Museum at Cooperstown, New York. For any baseball fan, the museum offers an exciting display of baseball — past and present.

Among the numerous displays, you will see a life-sized wood sculpture of Babe Ruth, the Hall of Fame Gallery where each Hall of Famer is represented by a bronze plaque, and over 1000 personal artifacts, photographs and memorabilia which present the history of the game. One of the most interesting exhibits shows the evolution of baseball equipment. The bats, balls, gloves and catchers' equipment of today are very different from what baseball's first players used. There is also an area devoted to Black baseball, where special recognition is given to the many contributions made by the early Negro leagues. There is a Ballparks Room, a World Series Room and a Playoff and Championship Series display. If you're a baseball-card collector, the museum has a unique collection of historic baseball cards.

These are just a few of the things to see at the Hall of Fame and Museum. I strongly recommend the trip to Cooperstown.

HALL OF FAME GALLERY. Each Hall of Famer is represented by a bronze plaque. Almost 200 baseball greats are immortalized here. It is the highest honor a baseball player can achieve.

Pre-1900   1910

TOBACCO AND GUM CARD DISPLAY.
This exhibit consists of over 900 different cards dating back to 1887.

BABE RUTH CARVING.
This is a life-sized sculpture
of Babe Ruth at age 34.
It weighs 300 pounds.

Courtesy of: THE NATIONAL BASEBALL HALL OF FAME AND MUSEUM. Cooperstown, N.Y. 13326

TEN
HALL OF FAMERS

WHO AM I?

Here are descriptions of
ten Hall of Famers and
Pictures of their plaques
at Cooperstown.
Can you guess who they are?

Answers on page 95

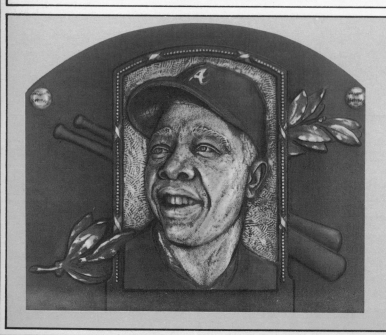

1

I spent 22 years (1954–76) with the
Braves, both in Milwaukee and
Atlanta, plus two seasons for the
Brewers. I became baseball's all-
time home-run king with a total of
755 four-baggers.

Hank Aaron
Answer

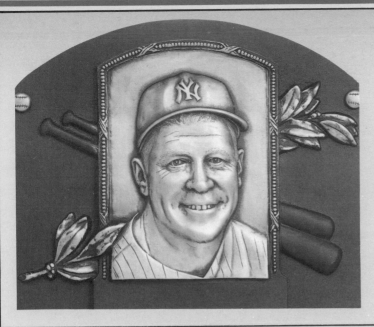

2

I played for the Yankees my entire career (1951–68). I led the American League in homers four times and hit more than 50 two times. I won the Triple Crown in 1956 and three times was named the league's Most Valuable Player.

_____
Answer

3

In 22 years (1951–1973) playing for the Giants and Mets, I hit 660 home runs, including four in one game. I drove in 100 or more runs eight seasons from 1959 through 1966.

_____
Answer

4

I was the last player to hit .400 (.406 in 1941). While playing 19 seasons for the Red Sox, I hit 521 home runs. Six times I led the league in batting before retiring in 1960 with a lifetime .344 batting average.

_____
Answer

5

I began as a lefthanded pitcher for the Red Sox in 1914. It was as an outfielder for the Yankees from 1920 through 1934 that I hit most of my 714 career home runs, including 60 in the 1927 season.

Babe Ruth

Answer

6

My .367 career batting average, compiled over 23 years with the Tigers and Philadelphia A's, from 1905 to 1928, is the highest ever recorded in modern times. I won a record dozen batting titles, including nine in a row from 1907 to 1915. Pete Rose broke my all-time hit record of 4,191 in 1985.

Answer

7

I won eight National League batting titles playing for the Pirates from 1900 to 1917. I finished with a .329 career batting average and am considered baseball's all-time shortstop. My baseball card has been sold for $35,000 and is considered the most valuable of all baseball cards.

Answer

8

The 511 games I won pitching in both leagues from 1890 to 1911 is a long-standing record. From 1891 through 1904, I won more than 20 games a season, including five in which I won 30 or more. There is an award named after me for the best pitchers in the American and National leagues.

_____
Answer

9

I won 20 or more games for the Giants in 13 of my 17 National League seasons, including 12 straight from 1903 to 1914. My 37 victories in 1908 remains the league record for most wins in one season.

_____
Answer

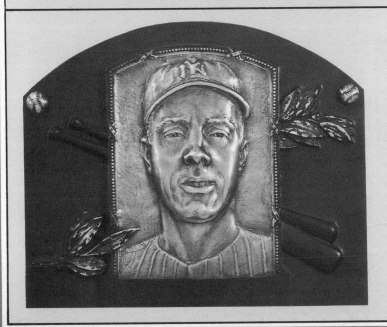

10

My 56-game hitting streak in 1941 is a record. In 11 of 13 active seasons from 1936 to 1951 with the Yankees, I batted over .300. I have a .325 lifetime batting average.

_____
Answer

FUTURE HALL OF FAMERS

★★★ *Red's Pick* ★★★

The following is by no means a complete list of all the present-day players with a chance to gain the Hall of Fame when their playing careers have ended. Some, such as Wade Boggs, the American League's perennial batting titlist and career .300 hitter, have been omitted because the position they play (third base in the case of Boggs) is handled by another candidate.

DON MATTINGLY: Consistency is the name of the game.

1B

RYNE SANDBERG: Ask National League managers if they'd like to have him.

2B

ALAN TRAMMELL: Does it year after year and without fanfare.

SS

MIKE SCHMIDT: Makes it on career homers alone.

 3B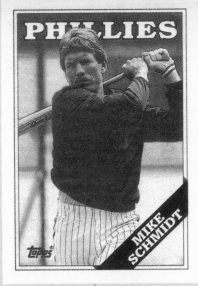

DARRYL STRAWBERRY: Has unlimited talent, future's up to him.

OF

TONY GWYNN: His .300 seasons keep adding up.

OF

JOSE CANSECO: Home-run and longball ability is unmatched.

OF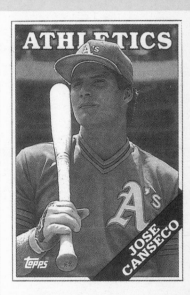

CARLTON FISK: Longevity plus defensive talents in his favor.

 C

NOLAN RYAN: Being the all-time strikeout king can't be discounted.

 P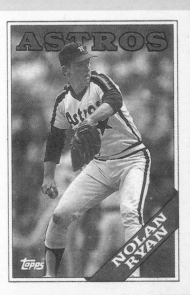

TRIVIA QUIZ

ATLANTA
BRAVES

Answers on page 94
Place stickers on opposite page

1. Annually among the league's best in home runs and RBIs, this popular veteran is the big bat in the Braves' batting order. He was the league's MVP in 1982 and 1983.

2. This southpaw, despite not posting big and fancy pitching numbers, is coveted by many major league clubs. Drafted by the Braves in June 1982, he has been a staff member since 1984.

3. One of baseball's all-time star relief pitchers, this veteran righthander made a remarkable comeback last year after sitting out most of 1986 and all of the 1987 season with a bad arm.

4. The Braves' No. 1 catcher the past three years, this righthanded hitter was originally signed by the Phillies in June 1976. He hit a career high 27 homers for Atlanta in 1987.

5. A candidate for the NL batting crown last year, this lefthanded-hitting first baseman is also a genuine threat to steal a base. He was the Braves' only representative in the 1988 All Star game.

Answers:

1 _____

2 _____

3 _____

4 _____

5 _____

TRIVIA QUIZ

CINCINNATI
REDS

Answers on page 94
Place stickers on opposite page

1. Always among the best in saves, this left-hander has been the key to the Reds' relief corps since 1984. Last year he reached the 100 plateau in career saves.

2. Another of the former Olympians to star in the majors, this righthand-hitting shortstop improved his batting average and stolen-base totals in 1988.

3. A righthand-hitting catcher who spent seven seasons in the minors for the Red Sox, he also played for the Indians and Phillies before being dealt to Cincinnati in August 1985.

4. A stolen-base and powerhitting threat, this lefthanded-swinging outfielder slumped a bit at the plate after his .334 season in 1987. Still he's regarded as one of the Reds' future stars.

5. A righthand-hitting outfielder, this fellow drove in 100 runs and stole 50 bases for Cincinnati in 1987. He dipped a bit at bat last year, but retains the talent to fulfill previous promise.

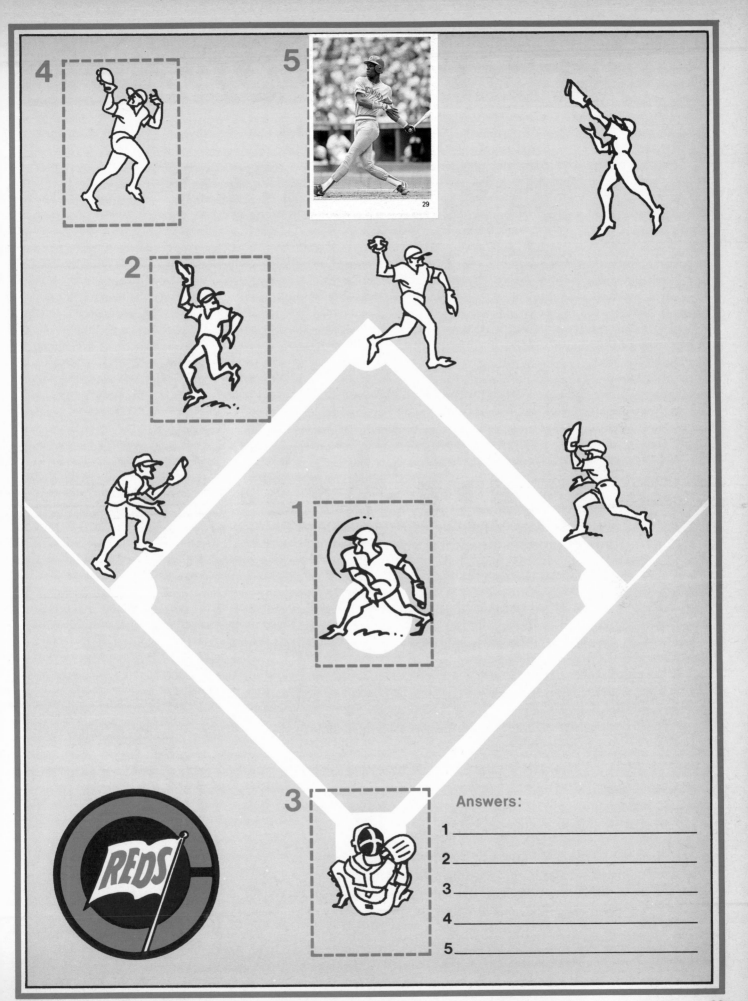

4

5

2

1

3

REDS

Answers:

1 _____

2 _____

3 _____

4 _____

5 _____

TRIVIA QUIZ

HOUSTON
ASTROS

Answers on page 94
Place stickers on opposite page

1. Baseball's all-time strikeout king, this veteran righthander has also authored a record five no-hitters. He has led the league in strikeouts nine times.

2. A so-so pitcher with the Mets, he mastered the split-finger delivery after moving to Houston and since 1985 has been one of the Astros' leading hurlers. He won the Cy Young Award in 1986.

3. This righthand-swinging first baseman is usually the Astros' leader in homers and RBIs. On September 10, 1987, he hit three homers in a game against the Padres in San Diego.

4. This switchhitting infielder is one of Houston's most valuable performers. A fine fielding second baseman, he's a timely hitter who can steal a base when needed.

5. This switchhitting veteran catcher performed for Cleveland and Toronto before joining the Astros in 1979. He has been the catcher in three no-hit performances by Houston pitchers.

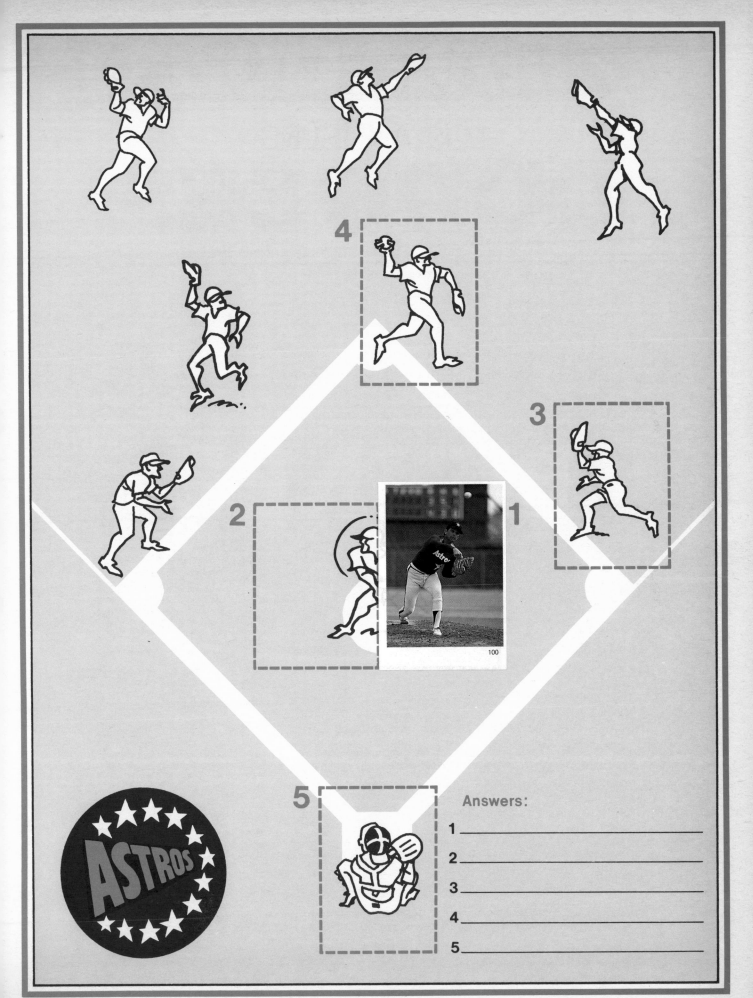

Answers:

1 _____

2 _____

3 _____

4 _____

5 _____

LOS ANGELES
DODGERS

Answers on page 94
Place stickers on opposite page

1. Considered the big bopper in the Dodgers' lineup since 1980, this righthand-hitting Dominican missed most of the 1986 season with a leg injury. After playing 11 seasons for the Dodgers, he was traded to the Cardinals in August, 1988.

2. Signed as a free agent by the Dodgers following a starry career in Detroit, this lefthanded powerhitter is a valid base stealer as well. He was an All America wide receiver at Michigan State.

3. The Dodgers' regular second baseman the past seven years, this righthand-hitting speedster was the Rookie of the Year in 1982. He batted .332 for the Dodgers in 1986.

4. A 19-game winner in 1985, this righthander is among the most sought after hurlers in the game. He has pitched over 200 innings in each of the past four seasons and won double figures in each.

5. Arm problems hampered him in 1988. But prior to that he was among the Dodgers' hill leaders since his sensational rookie season in 1981. For six years he exceeded 250 innings pitched and struck out 200 or more in three of those seasons.

2

3

1

5

4

Answers:

1 _____

2 _____

3 _____

4 _____

5 _____

TRIVIA QUIZ

SAN DIEGO
PADRES

Answers on page 94
Place stickers on opposite page

1. Used at first as well as in the outfield, this lefty swinger hit over .300 in four minor league seasons. He did likewise for San Diego in 1986 and 1987.

2. Definitely one of baseball's finest hitters, this lefthand-batting outfielder has batted over .300 for six straight years. He won three NL batting titles and three times collected more than 200 base hits.

3. The National League's Rookie of the Year in 1987, this righthand-batting catcher is estimated to have one of the finest throwing arms in baseball. After batting safely in 34 straight games in 1987, his average and power dipped last year.

4. A switchhitting second baseman, he batted .346 and .319 in his final two minor league seasons. The son of a former major leaguer, his younger brother is rated one of the top catching prospects in the minors.

5. Traded by the Giants to the Padres in July 1987, this lefthanded reliever became *Numero Uno* in the San Diego bullpen last season. Originally signed by the Phillies in 1979, he was dealt to San Francisco in December 1972.

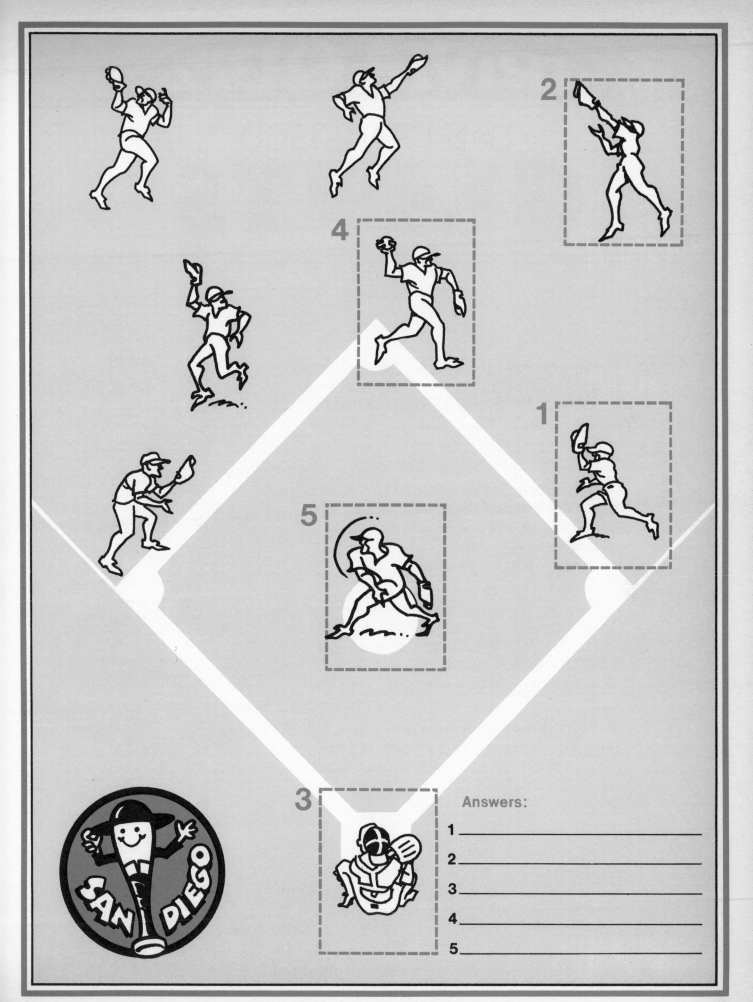

Answers:

1 _____
2 _____
3 _____
4 _____
5 _____

TRIVIA QUIZ

SAN FRANCISCO
GIANTS

Answers on page 94
Place stickers on opposite page

1. Last year was his third with the Giants, but in that time this righthand-hitting infielder has earned respect from his NL peers. His batting average rose in 1988 and he has shown he can steal bases.

2. Originally property of the Dodgers, he was dealt to the Giants in December 1985 and has become one of their steadiest outfielders. A righthanded batter, he hit 38 homers in his first two seasons in San Francisco.

3. A former Olympian, this lefthand-hitting first baseman has shown power and RBI ability. Along with hitting a homer in his first major league at bat in 1986, he made the All Star squad last year.

4. This righthander pitched for the Reds, Astros and Royals before joining the Giants in 1986. Since that time he has been a regular in their mound rotation.

5. An important addition to the Giants' bullpen the past four years, this righthander was originally signed by the Giants in 1979 and worked his way through their system to the big club in 1983.

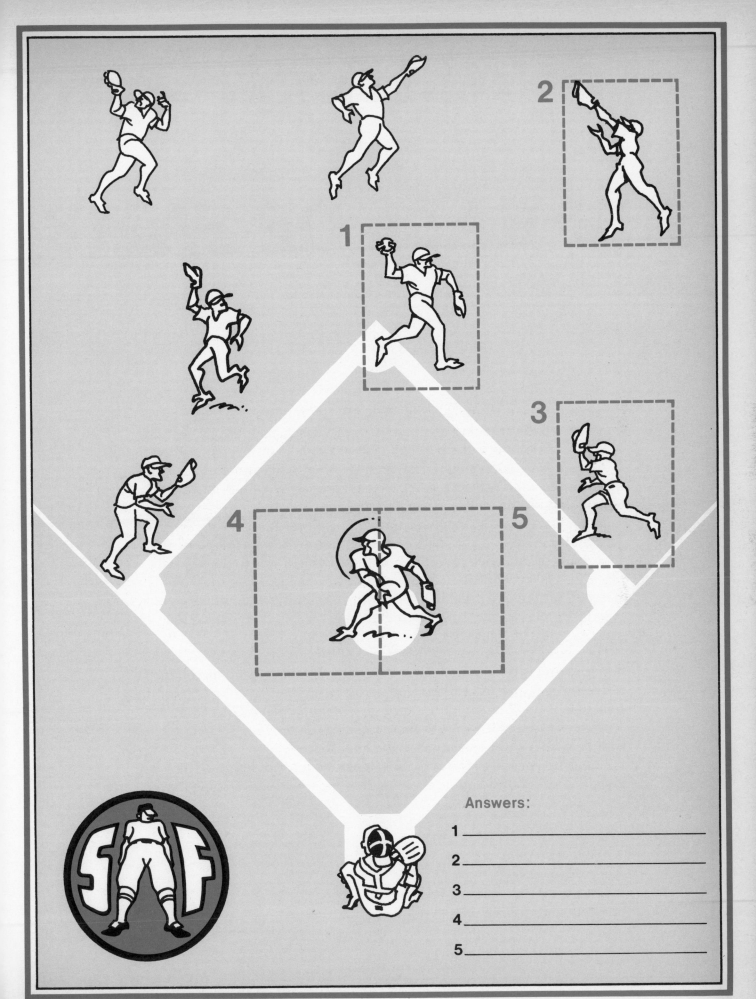

Answers:

1 _____

2 _____

3 _____

4 _____

5 _____

GETTING ELECTED TO THE HALL OF FAME

Batting titles, pitching awards, World Series honors and lucrative contracts are desired and acceptable, but it's every ballplayer's ultimate aim to win election to the baseball Hall of Fame.

A plaque at Cooperstown, however, requires skills and abilities endowed to what amounts to a precious few. Many ballplayers are considered for the Hall of Fame, but few are chosen.

To qualify as a Cooperstown candidate, a player must have performed for at least ten seasons and must wait five years following retirement as an active player to become eligible. Prior to the annual election, players eligible for the first time are evaluated by the Baseball Writers Association of America's Screening Committee, which weeds out players whose only credential is the fact they played ten seasons without otherwise distinguishing themselves.

The voting is conducted by the Baseball Writers Association of America and is done only by those writers who have been members for ten or more years. To gain the Hall, a candidate must receive 75% of the total vote in any one election. Once on a ballot, a player, providing he continues to get at least 5% of the total vote, remains on the ballot for fifteen elections unless elected to the Hall sooner.

Voters are permitted to cast ballots for up to ten candidates. They can vote for fewer, but not more than ten. Unlike the Most Valuable Player award, in which the order of selection creates a point total, each Hall of Fame vote counts as one.

As yet no one has ever been unanimously elected to the Hall, including the immortal Ty Cobb, one of the six originals selected in the first election in 1936. Cobb, despite 4,191 lifetime hits and a career .367 batting average, plus a dozen batting titles, missed by four votes from being unanimous.

Cobb appeared on 222 of the 226 ballots, winning 98% of the vote. Even the immensely popular Babe Ruth, whose home-run bat created the longball era that exists today, failed to appear on 11 of the original ballots. More recently, 23 failed to name Willie Mays, and 9 skipped Henry Aaron.

If a candidate fails to gain election from the BBWAA during his fifteen years on the ballot, he passes, following a three-year wait, to the Hall of Fame's Committee on Baseball Veterans. This is an eighteen-man committee consisting of former players, some club and league officials and long-time baseball writers. The Veterans Committee meets annually, usually in March, and can name two former players in any one year.

ALL TIME BASEBALL LEADERS
VS.
CURRENT CONTENDERS

There are several active major league baseball players with a chance to be record breakers. Listed are the top three record holders in these categories and the present day player who is contending.

BATTERS

MOST CONSECUTIVE GAMES

Leaders: Lou Gehrig (2,130);
Everett Scott (1,307); Steve Garvey (1,207)
Present Day Contender: *Cal Ripken Jr. (1,088)*

MOST LIFETIME HITS

Leaders: Pete Rose (4,256);
Ty Cobb (4,191); Henry Aaron (3,771)
Present Day Contender: *Bill Buckner (2,669)*

MOST TWO BASE HITS

Leaders: Tris Speaker (793);
Pete Rose (746); Stan Musial (725)
Present Day Contender: *Bill Buckner (494)*

MOST THREE BASE HITS

Leaders: Sam Crawford (312);
Ty Cobb (298); Honus Wagner (252)
Present Day Contender: *Willie Wilson (123)*

MOST HOME RUNS

Leaders: Henry Aaron (755);
Babe Ruth (714); Willie Mays (660)
Present Day Contender: *Mike Schmidt (542)*

MOST GRAND-SLAM HRs

Leaders: Lou Gehrig (23); Willie McCovey (18);
Jimmie Foxx (17); Ted Williams (17)
Present Day Contender: *Eddie Murray (14)*

MOST RBIs

Leaders: Henry Aaron (2,297);
Babe Ruth (2,204); Lou Gehrig (1,990)
Present Day Contender: *Mike Schmidt (1,567)*

MOST BASES ON BALLS

Leaders: Babe Ruth (2,056);
Ted Williams (2,019); Joe Morgan (1,865)
Present Day Contender: *Mike Schmidt (1,486)*

MOST STRIKEOUTS

Leaders: Reggie Jackson (2,597);
Willie Stargell (1,936); Tony Perez (1,867)

Present Day Contender: *Mike Schmidt (1,866)*

MOST STOLEN BASES

Leaders: Lou Brock (938);
Billy Hamilton (937); Ty Cobb (892)

Present Day Contender: *Rickey Henderson (794)*

PITCHERS

MOST GAMES

Leaders: Hoyt Wilhelm (1,070);
Lindy McDaniel (987); Rollie Fingers (944)

Present Day Contender: *Kent Tekulve (1,013)*

MOST STARTS

Leaders: Cy Young (818);
Don Sutton (756), Phil Niekro (716)

Present Day Contender: *Tommy John (690)*

MOST INNINGS PITCHED

Leaders: Cy Young (7,377);
Pud Galvin (5,959); Walter Johnson (5,923)
Present Day Contender: *Tommy John (4,643⅔)*

MOST VICTORIES

Leaders: Cy Young (511); Walter Johnson (416);
Christy Mathewson (373); Grover Alexander (373)
Present Day Contender: *Tommy John (286)*

MOST SAVES

Leaders: Rollie Fingers (341);
Rich Gossage (302); Bruce Sutter (300)

MOST SHUTOUTS

Leaders: Walter Johnson (110);
Grover Alexander (90); Christy Mathewson (83)
Present Day Contender: *Nolan Ryan (55)*

MOST BASES ON BALLS

Leaders: Nolan Ryan (2,442);
Steve Carlton (1,828); Phil Niekro (1,809)

MOST STRIKEOUTS

Leaders: Nolan Ryan (4,775)
Steve Carlton (4,131); Tom Seaver (3,640)

★ ★ ★   ★ ★ ★

TRIVIA QUIZ

BALTIMORE
ORIOLES

Answers on page 94
Place stickers on opposite page

1. A member of the All Star squad for six straight years, he's a former Rookie of the Year and an MVP. During the 1988 season his contract was renewed, indicating the Orioles hope to rebuild their club with him as one of the keys.

2. During his dozen years in Baltimore, this switchhitter has established more than a few batting records. He almost annually leads the Orioles in home runs and runs batted in.

3. The only man to win Rookie of the Year and MVP in the same season, this lefthanded-hitting outfielder won the American League batting crown with a .333 average in 1979. He was traded to Detroit in September 1988.

4. He spent five and a half seasons in the Orioles system before gaining a berth in the Birds' infield. Unlike his older brother he's not a powerhitter or RBI man, but serves well as a tablesetter.

5. Acquired from the Phillies for the 1988 season, this righthanded hitter's third-base play was overshadowed by teammate Mike Schmidt during his days in the National League.

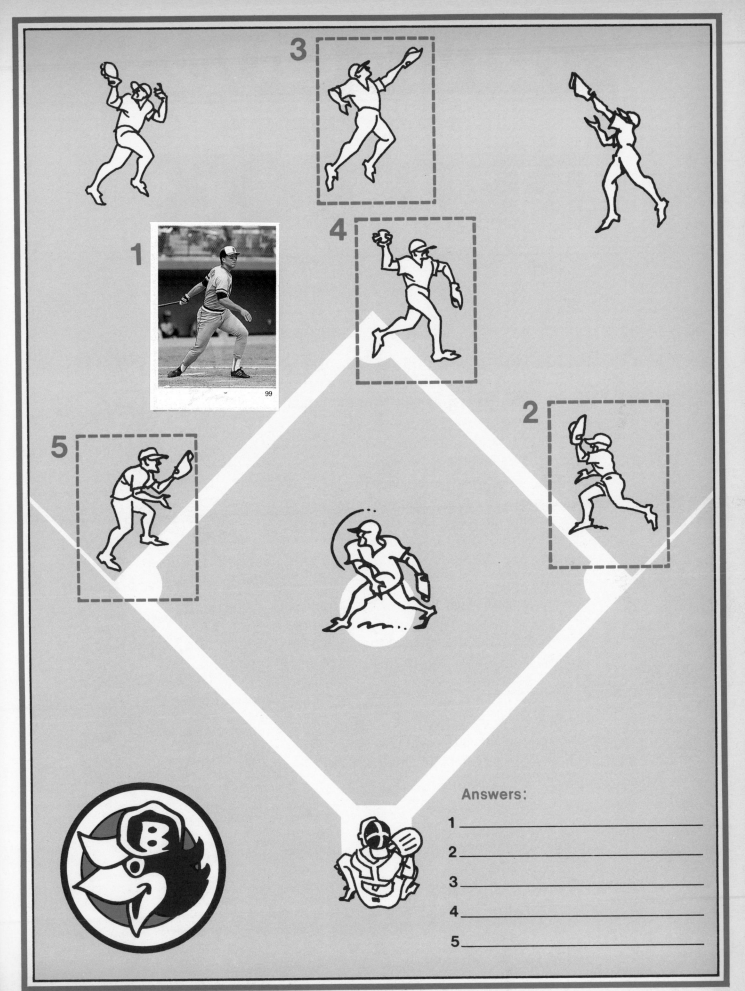

99

3

1

4

5

2

Answers:

1 _____

2 _____

3 _____

4 _____

5 _____

45

TRIVIA QUIZ

BOSTON
RED SOX

Answers on page 94
Place stickers on opposite page

1. The American League's strikeout king last year, this righthander fanned a record 20 Seattle batters on April 29, 1986. A perennial Cy Young candidate, he's a product of the University of Texas.

2. A longtime bullpen star in the National League, he moved to Boston last year and continued to display his relief talents. This big righthander has accumulated more than 200 major league saves.

3. In his 17 seasons with the Sox this righthanded slugger is No. 4 on the club's all-time home-run list. He switched from the outfield to first base in 1987 and the move didn't hamper him defensively.

4. A .300 lifetime hitter, this fellow has made a career of winning the American League batting title. He has done just that the past four seasons and in five of the last six.

5. His defensive prowess at shortstop is unquestioned. Though not a powerhitter, this 1988 rookie displayed his ability to make contact. As a result, striking him out is one of the pitcher's toughest jobs.

3

5

4

1

2

Answers:

1 _____

2 _____

3 _____

4 _____

5 _____

STICKER NUMBERS

On the next pages are the stickers for the answers to the Trivia Quizzes. This list shows the sticker numbers and each player's name.

1. Doyle Alexander		27. Al Davis
2. Luis Alicea		28. Chili Davis
3. Roberto Alomar		29. Eric Davis
4. Alan Ashby		30. Glen Davis
5. Floyd Bannister		31. Jody Davis
6. Jesse Barfield		32. Mark Davis
7. George Bell		33. Andre Dawson
8. Wade Boggs		34. Rob Deer
9. Barry Bonds		35. Jose Deleon
10. Bobby Bonilla		36. Bo Diaz
11. Chris Bosio		37. Bill Doran
12. George Brett		38. Shawon Dunston
13. Hubie Brooks		39. Dennis Eckersley
14. Tom Brunansky		40. Dwight Evans
15. Tim Burke		41. Tony Fernandez
16. Ivan Calderon		42. Brian Fisher
17. Tom Candiotti		43. Carlton Fisk
18. Jose Canseco		44. Mike Flanagan
19. Gary Carter		45. John Franco
20. Joe Carter		46. Gary Gaetti
21. Jack Clark		47. Andres Galarraga
22. Will Clark		48. Scott Garrelts
23. Roger Clemens		49. Kirk Gibson
24. David Cone		50. Dan Gladden
25. Ed Correa		51. Dwight Gooden
26. Kal Daniels		52. Pedro Guerrero

Continued on page 49

ANSWERS TO TRIVIA QUIZZES

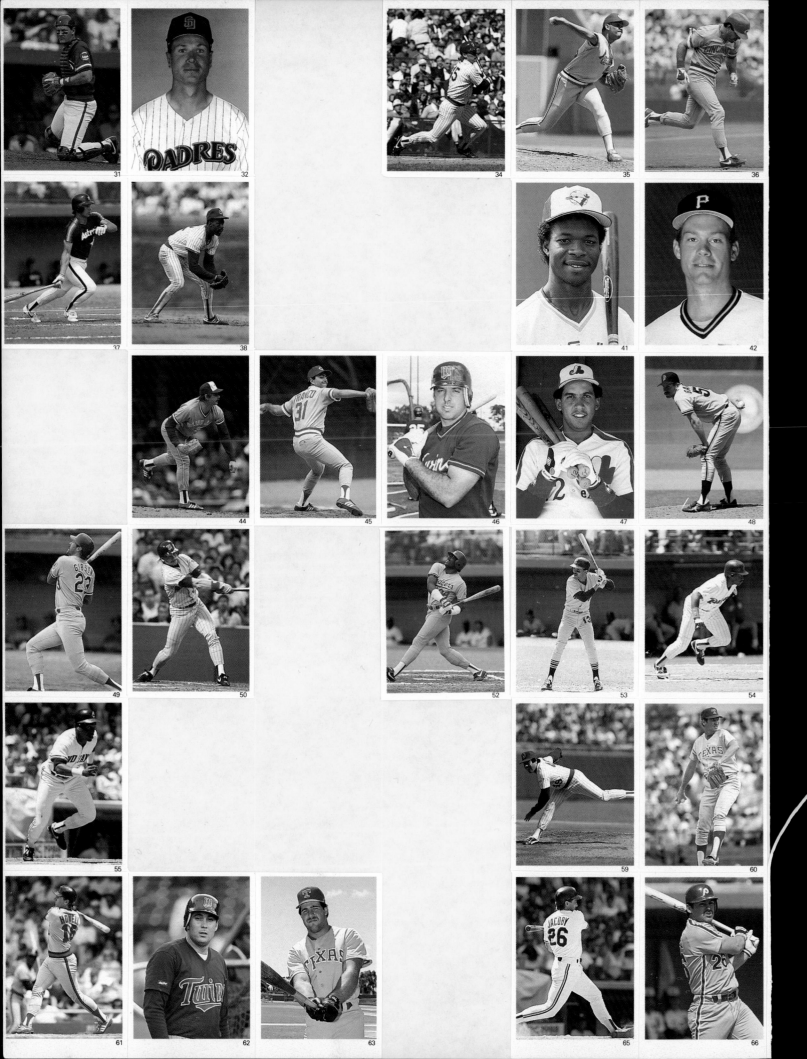

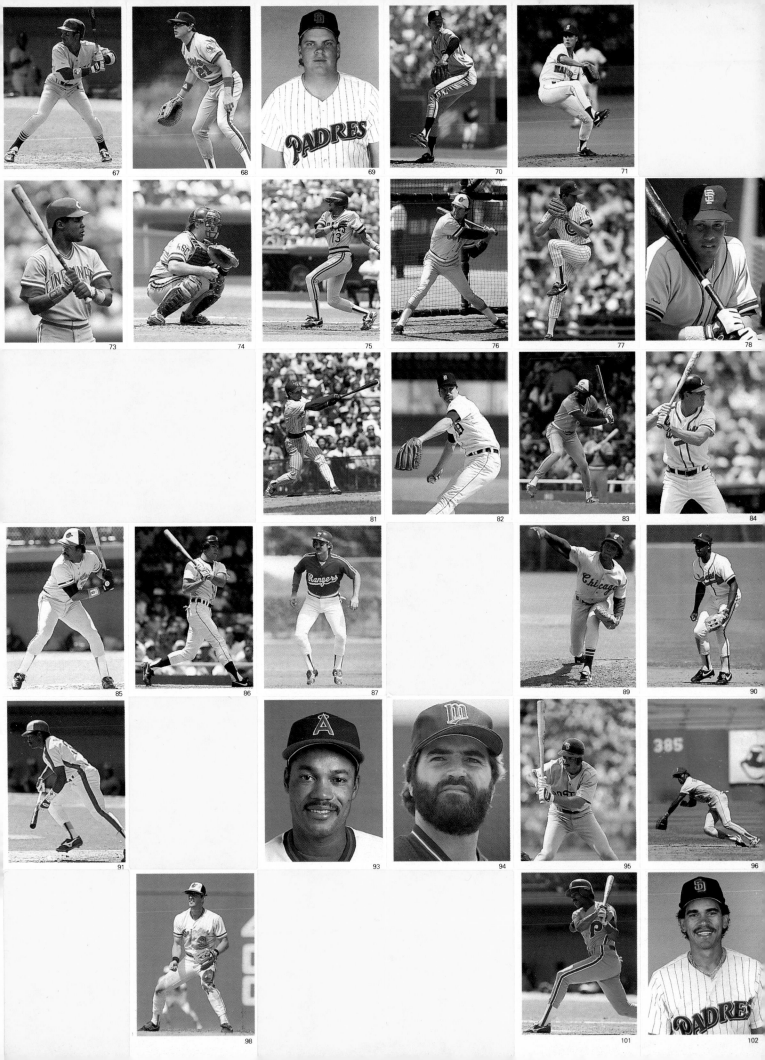

53. Ozzie Guillen	92. Willie Randolph
54. Tony Gwynn	93. Johnny Ray
55. Mel Hall	94. Jeff Reardon
56. Von Hayes	95. Jody Reed
57. Keith Hernandez	96. Harold Reynolds
58. Orel Hershiser	97. Dave Righetti
59. Ted Higuera	98. Billy Ripken
60. Charlie Hough	99. Cal Ripken, Jr.
61. Jack Howell	100. Nolan Ryan
62. Kent Hrbek	101. Juan Samuel
63. Pete Incaviglia	102. Benito Santiago
64. Bo Jackson	103. Steve Sax
65. Brook Jacoby	104. Mike Schmidt
66. Chris James	105. Rick Schu
67. Lance Johnson	106. Mike Scott
68. Wally Joyner	107. Kevin Seitzer
69. Jack Kruk	108. Ruben Sierra
70. Mike LaCoss	109. Lee Smith
71. Mark Langston	110. Ozzie Smith
72. Carney Lansford	111. Zane Smith
73. Barry Larkin	112. Dave Stewart
74. Mike LaValliere	113. Darryl Strawberry
75. Jose Lind	114. Bruce Sutter
76. Fred Lynn	115. Bill Swift
77. Greg Maddux	116. Gary Swindell
78. Candy Maldonado	117. Frank Tanana
79. Don Mattingly	118. Danny Tartabull
80. Mark McGwire	119. Milt Thompson
81. Paul Molitor	120. Rob Thompson
82. Jack Morris	121. Alan Trammell
83. Lloyd Moseby	122. John Tudor
84. Dale Murphy	123. Fernando Valenzuela
85. Eddie Murray	124. Dave Valle
86. Matt Nokes	125. Frank Viola
87. Pete O'Brien	126. Ozzie Virgil
88. Rafael Palmeiro	127. Tim Wallach
89. Melido Perez	128. Dave Winfield
90. Gerald Perry	129. Mike Witt
91. Tim Raines	130. Robin Yount

TRIVIA QUIZ

CLEVELAND
INDIANS

Answers on page 94
Place stickers on opposite page

1. This former Cubs outfielder has proven a genuine RBI threat for Cleveland. He led the AL with 121 RBIs in 1986. Along with his longball ability he's a fine basestealer.

2. His home-run production slipped a bit in 1988, but this infielder has been one of the Indians' more prominent performers since being acquired from Atlanta following the 1983 season.

3. He was one of the league's top lefthanded pitchers early in the 1988 season before experiencing a mound slump. But this former U. of Texas hurler showed signs of recovery following the All Star game break.

4. His ability to master the difficult knuckleball enabled this righthander to reach success after seven minor league seasons. He won 16 for Cleveland in 1986.

5. A part of the seven-player trade the Indians made with the Cubs in June, 1984, this lefthanded batter has found a home in the Cleveland outfield.

50

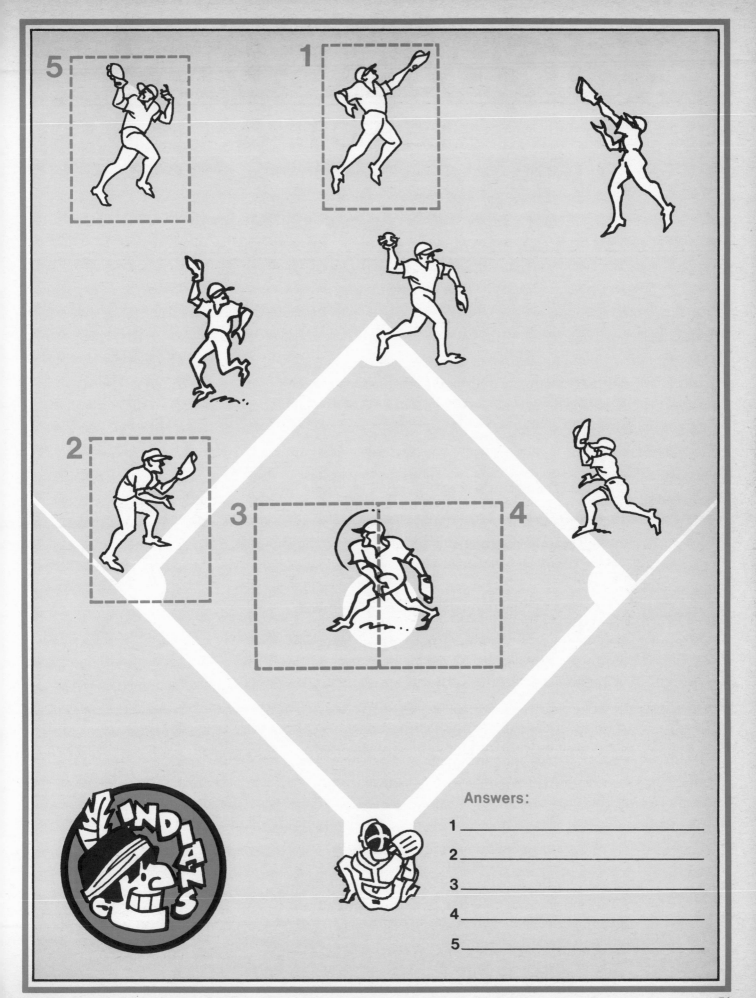

Answers:

1 _____

2 _____

3 _____

4 _____

5 _____

TRIVIA QUIZ

DETROIT
TIGERS

Answers on page 94
Place stickers on opposite page

1. Used both as a catcher and designated hitter, this lefty swinger continued to display his longball abilities again in 1988. As a rookie with Detroit he not only made the All Star squad but hit 32 homers during the 1987 season.

2. One of the game's top performers for many years, he has been considered the "heart" of the Tigers' infield for a dozen years. In 1984 his two homers and .450 batting average earned him the MVP prize in the World Series.

3. A veteran of eight major league clubs in both leagues, this righthander broke in with the Dodgers in 1971. He joined Detroit from Atlanta in August 1987 and paced the Tigers to the division title with a 9–0 record.

4. One of the game's top pitching workhorses for the past decade, this righthander twice won 20 games, was an All Star pitcher four times and won two World Series games for the victorious Tigers in 1984.

5. A former fireballer when he pitched for California in the early 1970s, this lefthander also pitched for the Red Sox and Rangers. He joined the Tigers in June 1985 and has been in their rotation ever since. He has won in double figures in 11 of his 16 major league seasons.

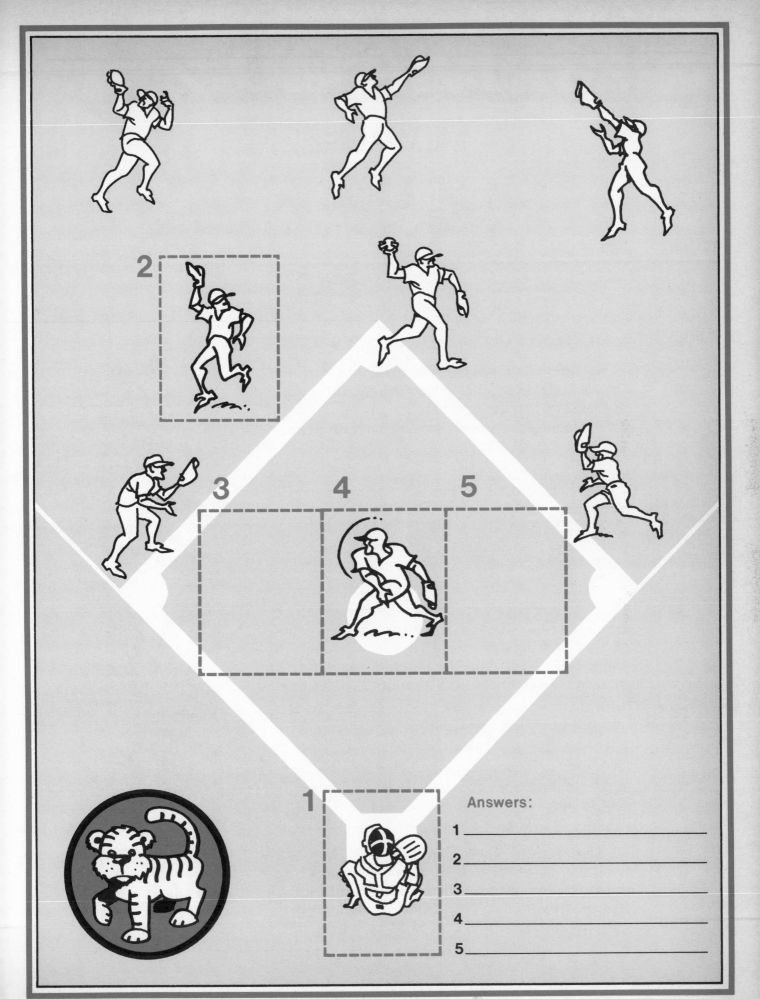

Answers:

1 _____

2 _____

3 _____

4 _____

5 _____

☆☆☆ TRIVIA QUIZ ☆☆☆

MILWAUKEE
BREWERS

Answers on page 94
Place stickers on opposite page

1. A .300 hitter for the second straight season, this versatile veteran has played second, third, the outfield and as a designated hitter. In addition he's always among the Brewers leaders in stolen bases.

2. Among Milwaukee's best since breaking in as an 18-year-old shortstop in 1974, he became an outfielder in recent seasons. The American League's MVP in 1982, he hit .300 the past three years.

3. Acquired from the Giants in December 1985, he has given the Brewers home-run sock. Though prone to striking out — he led the AL with a record 186 in 1987 — this outfielder also tied a mark for grand-slam homers in successive games in August 1987.

4. This Mexican lefthander is an accomplished pitcher. A 20-game winner in 1986, his walks-to-strikeout ratio is annually among the leaders. He was a member of the American League's All Star staff in 1986.

5. Despite a losing record in 1988, this right-hander, who spent five seasons in the Brewers minor league system, is still considered a future winner. He won 11 in 1987 and was stalled by arm ailments last year.

54

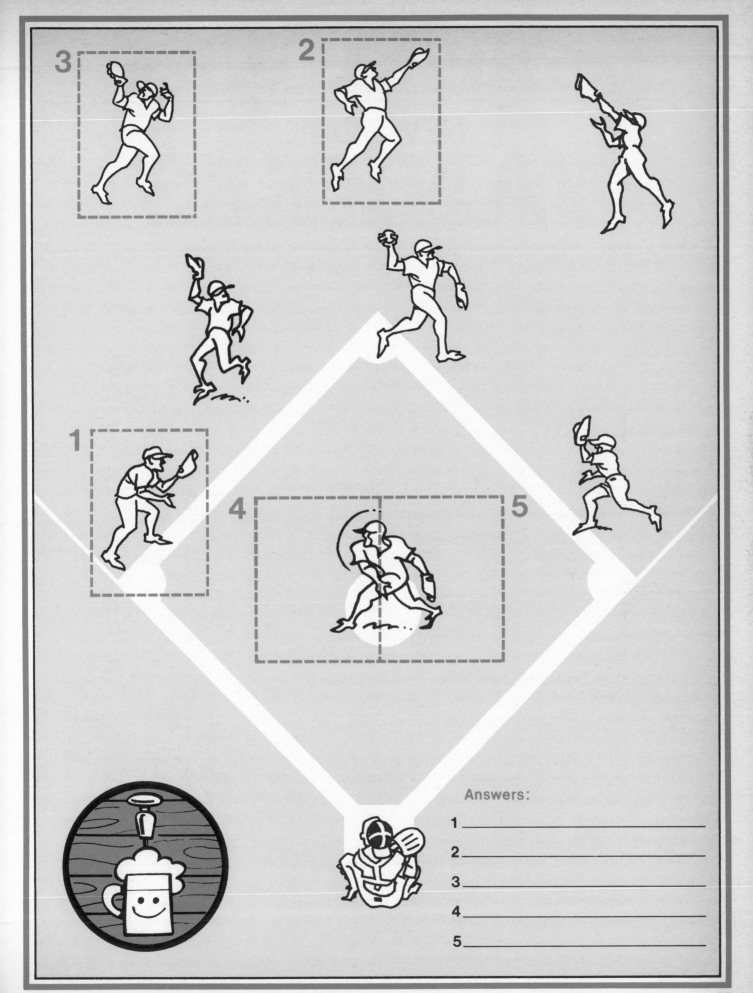

Answers:

1 _____

2 _____

3 _____

4 _____

5 _____

TRIVIA QUIZ

NEW YORK
YANKEES

Answers on page 94
Place stickers on opposite page

1. He had 100 or more RBIs in each season from 1982 through 1986. A member of the All Star team in both leagues for 12 straight years, this fellow was drafted out of college by professional baseball, football and basketball clubs.

2. Author of a no-hitter in 1983, he shifted to the bullpen the following year and has been among the best relievers ever since. The AL Rookie of the Year in 1981, this lefthander had a record 46 saves in 1986.

3. Signed as a free agent prior to the 1988 season, he's remembered for a three-run homer against the Dodgers that gave St. Louis the 1985 NL flag. Formerly an outfielder with the Giants, he played first base for St. Louis before becoming a designated hitter last year.

4. Acquired from Pittsburgh in December 1975, this player has long been considered the glue of the Yankees infield. A .305 hitter in 1987, he was bothered by injuries which hampered him at the plate last season.

5. A lifetime .300 hitter, he won the AL batting title with a .343 in 1984. In 1987 he set a record by hitting six grand-slam homers. One of the best fielders in baseball, this fellow has made the All Star team the past five seasons.

1

128

4

92

5

79

2

97

3

21

Answers:

1 Dave winfield

2 Dave r.

3 Jack Clark

4 _____

5 _____

TRIVIA QUIZ

TORONTO
BLUE JAYS

Answers on page 94
Place stickers on opposite page

1. Signed at 17, this switchhitting Dominican infielder hit .300 in both 1986 and 1987. Many regard him as the finest shortstop in the American League. He owns the Jays club record for RBIs in one season by a switchhitter.

2. Despite problems with management in 1988, this righthand-hitting outfielder and designated hitter was the American League's MVP in 1987. He had over 100 runs batted in each of the 1986 and 1987 seasons and hit a total of 78 homers during those two years.

3. This veteran southpaw, a 20-game winner for Baltimore in 1979, joined Toronto in August 1987. Last year he pitched consistently for the Jays. Still a workhorse, in six seasons for the Orioles he exceeded 200 innings pitched.

4. A longball hitter and stolen-base threat, this lefty-swinging outfielder has been a regular in the Toronto lineup since 1980. He's the club's all-time leader in games played, stolen bases and basehits.

5. His throwing arm makes him one of the finest outfielders in the game. In addition he has power and accounts for RBIs. He underwent off-season surgery on his wrist and knee prior to 1988, and it limited his output a bit last year.

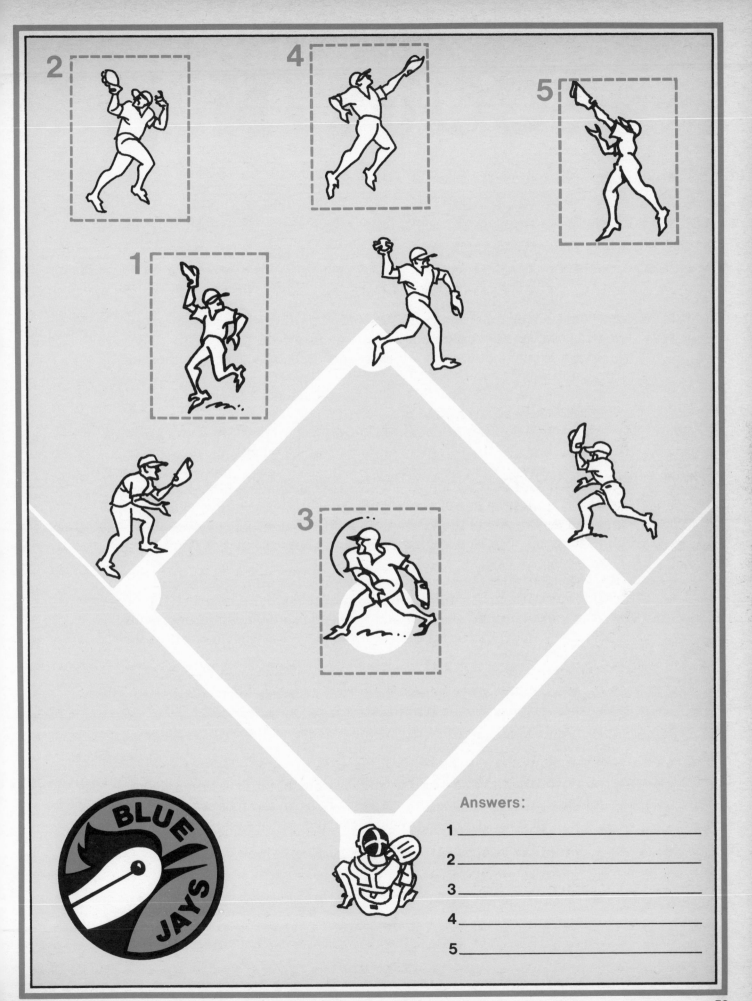

Answers:

1 _____

2 _____

3 _____

4 _____

5 _____

SCOUTING

Young ballplayers, particularly at the high school level, have a fear that no one will notice them and as a result they'll never get the chance to advance into professional baseball. It shouldn't be a worry because modern scouting methods do not permit a boy to go unseen.

Major league scouts and their assistants constantly watch sandlot, high school and college games, and any lad with playing skill and ability will be scouted. He may not realize that fact, but somewhere and someplace he'll be spotted and a report turned in.

Scouts and their representatives, known as bird dogs, find prospects in the remotest places. In fact, there have been times when a player, even as a young teenager, has been spotted. That's exactly what happened with Harold Baines of the Chicago White Sox. He was playing Little League ball in his native, Easton, Maryland, and the late Bill Veeck, then an Easton resident and later owner of the White Sox, spotted Baines. He followed the youngster's advance, and in June 1977 Harold became the Sox's No. 1 pick in the free-agent draft.

The majors invest huge sums of money in their farm systems and development programs, and scouting is the lifeblood of the game. The people who look at untried and untested youngsters are known as free-agent scouts. They watch high school and college players as well as those in such amateur programs as the American Legion.

The scouts are constantly searching for young pitchers with "live" arms and boys who show power at the plate. They also seek kids with defense skills, since in today's game running speed is a valuable asset.

In addition to free-agent scouts, major league clubs assign people to watch rival teams, particularly in the minors. Their assignment is to seek out talented players who might be available to help the scout's particular club and who might be acquired in trades. Many of today's clubs assign a scout to travel ahead of his team. He's known as an advance scout and his duty is to determine who is hot, who is not and which opposing player is hurt.

Many of them chart virtually every pitch in a major league game and determine which players hit which particular pitch and which of them will steal a base and which of them will use the hit-and-run. As a result, the charts compiled will enable the manager of the scout's team to set up a defense against each and every opposing player.

Clubs also employ scouts to watch other teams to possibly determine whether someone on that club could fit into the scout's organization. Many post-season deals are made at the major league level on the strength of what a scout has seen during his travels that season.

However, the majority of scouts still work in the free-agent field, looking for amateurs who are prospects. Scouts spend countless hours searching for kids who display the talent that might possibly carry them from the corner sandlot to the major leagues.

So if you have any playing ability it will not go unnoticed. If you keep playing, sooner or later a scout will spot you, and if he likes what he sees then you too may get the opportunity to fulfill the dream of someday playing major league baseball.

Here is an actual scouting-report form used to evaluate a future pitcher. Fill in the blanks the way you think a scout would write about you.

OVERALL FUTURE POTENTIAL: **REPORT NO:**

PLAYER: **POSITION:**

CURRENT ADDRESS:

TELEPHONE: **DATE OF BIRTH:**

HEIGHT: **WEIGHT:**   **BATS:**   **THROWS:**

PERMANENT ADDR:

TEAM NAME:

SCOUT: **DATE:**   **GAMES:**

RATING KEY...   **INN:**

        8 — OUTSTANDING   4 — BELOW AVERAGE
        7 — VERY GOOD   3 — WELL BELOW AVG
        6 — ABOVE AVERAGE   2 — POOR
        5 — AVERAGE

PITCHERS   **PRES**   **FUT**

FASTBALL .7 6 . . . .   HABITS . . . .
CURVE .6 .7 . . . .   DEDICATION . . . .
CONTROL . .6 6 . .   AGILITY . . . .
CHANGE OF PACE 6 8   APTITUDE . . . .
SLIDER .6 6 7   PHYS. MATURITY . . . .
KNUCKLEBALL . .7 . .   EMOT. MATURITY . . . .
OTHER 5 8 . . . . .   MARRIED . . . .
POISE 7 . . . .
BASEBALL INSTINCT 8 8   DATE ELIGIBLE . . . .
AGGRESSIVENESS 8 7   PHASE . . . .

ARM ACTION
DELIVERY
<u>PHYSICAL DESCRIPTION:</u>

<u>ABILITIES:</u>

<u>WEAKNESS:</u>

<u>SUMMATION AND SIGNABILITY:</u>

Here is an actual scouting-report form used to evaluate a future batter. Fill in the blanks the way you think a scout would write about you.

OVERALL FUTURE POTENTIAL: **REPORT NO:**

PLAYER: **POSITION:**

CURRENT ADDRESS:

TELEPHONE: **DATE OF BIRTH:**

HEIGHT: **WEIGHT:**   **BATS:**   **THROWS:**

PERMANENT ADDR:

TEAM NAME:

SCOUT: **DATE:**   **GAMES:**

RATING KEY...   **INN:**

8 — OUTSTANDING	4 — BELOW AVERAGE
7 — VERY GOOD	3 — WELL BELOW AVG
6 — ABOVE AVERAGE	2 — POOR
5 — AVERAGE	

NON-PITCHERS   **PRES**   **FUT**

HITTING ABILITY *7* *5*   HABITS . . . .
POWER *8* *6* . . . . .   DEDICATION . . . .
RUNNING SPEED *9* *5*   AGILITY . . . .
BASE RUNNING *8* *7*   APTITUDE . . . .
ARM STRENGTH . *7* *8*   PHYS. MATURITY . . . .
ARM ACCURACY *6* *8*   EMOT. MATURITY . . . .
FIELDING *6* *7* *5*   MARRIED . . . .
RANGE *6* . . . . *8* . .
BASEBALL INSTINCT *8* *8*   DATE ELIGIBLE . . . .
AGGRESSIVENESS *8* *8*   PHASE . . . .

PHYSICAL DESCRIPTION:

ABILITIES:

WEAKNESSES:

SUMMATION AND SIGNABILITY:

ROOKIES NOT BOTHERED BY THE

"SOPHOMORE JINX"

The following is a list of rookies, many of whom won the Rookie of the Year award in their first year and then went on to prove it was no fluke by having an even better second year in the majors. These are rookies who weren't bothered by what is called the "Sophomore Jinx".

CARLTON FISK

Carlton Fisk, then with Boston, was the AL's Rookie of the Year in 1972 and the next season improved his home-run and RBI totals.

EDDIE MURRAY ### ANDRE DAWSON

In 1977 Eddie Murray (Baltimore) and Andre Dawson (Montreal) were the Rookie of the Year winners. The next season Murray hit for a higher batting average and increased his RBI numbers. Dawson bettered his home-run and RBI numbers as a sophomore.

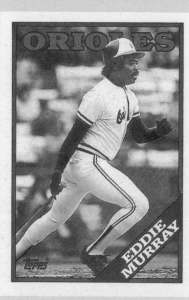

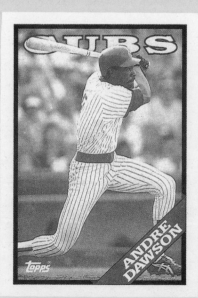

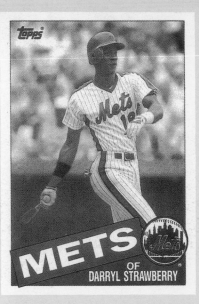

BOB HORNER

Bob Horner was the NL's Rookie winner in 1978 for the Braves and in his second year increased his batting average 48 points to .314 and hit 10 more homers and got 35 more RBIs.

CAL RIPKEN

Cal Ripken, Jr., was the AL's Rookie of the Year in 1982 and the following year he led the Orioles to the World Series and was the American League's Most Valuable Player.

DARRYL STRAWBERRY

The Mets' Darryl Strawberry was the NL's rookie winner in 1983 and in 1984 continued to be a longball and RBI man.

DWIGHT GOODEN

In 1984 the baseball world went gaga over the Mets' Dwight Gooden, and as a sophomore he won 24 games and pitched to a 1.53 earned run average after being 17–9 and 2.60 as a freshman.

JOSE CANSECO

Oakland's Jose Canseco was the first-year sensation in 1986 and the next season continued his longball antics.

MARK McGWIRE

In 1987 the A's celebrated Mark McGwire was the AL's top freshman. Last year his output was enough to get him elected to the American League All Star squad for the second straight season.

CALIFORNIA
ANGELS

Answers on page 94
Place stickers on opposite page

1. A big home-run threat in 1986 and 1987, this lefthanded hitter finally rediscovered his longball touch following last year's All Star break. He was the Angels' third pick in the June 1983 free-agent draft.

2. Still remembered for his perfect game against Texas in September 1984, this righthander has pitched for the Angels since 1981. He got off slowly last year and as a result wasn't picked for the All Star team after being selected in 1986 and 1987.

3. This switchhitter made a remarkable recovery for the Angels last year. Obtained from Pittsburgh, for whom he played seven years, in August 1987, he was one of California's most consistent performers in 1988.

4. Signed by the Angels as a free agent in December 1987, this former San Francisco outfielder didn't allow the change of leagues to bother his play. A switchhitter, he's consistent with his home runs and RBIs.

5. Used both as an infielder and outfielder, this lefty-swinging product of the University of Arizona had some good minor league seasons in the Angels' system before establishing his spot in the regular lineup.

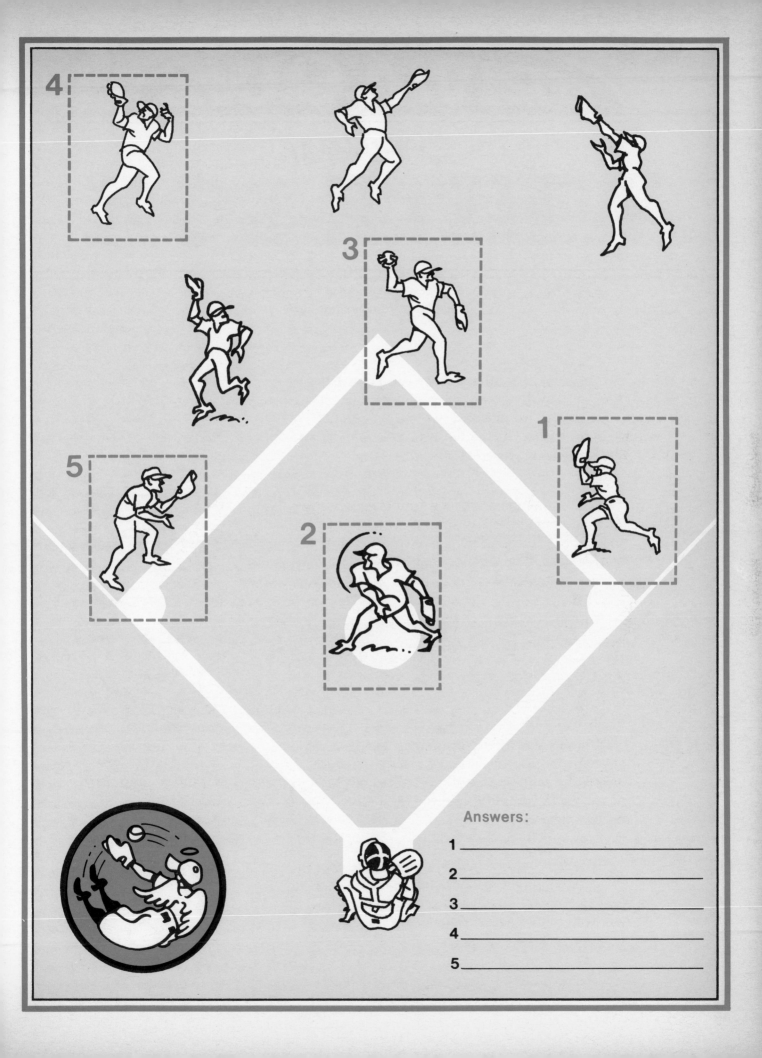

Answers:

1 _____

2 _____

3 _____

4 _____

5 _____

CHICAGO
WHITE SOX

Answers on page 94
Place stickers on opposite page

1. This rookie righthander was one of the brighter spots in the White Sox's pitching rotation last summer. Obtained from Kansas City in December 1987, his older brother formerly pitched for the Braves before going to Montreal.

2. A hand injury kept this future Hall of Fame candidate out of the Sox' lineup until late July, 1988. One of the few catchers to hit 300 home runs, he was the AL's Rookie of the Year in 1972.

3. His 1988 season was cut short by a shoulder problem in July, but prior to that his home-run and RBI production was among the White Sox's leaders in those categories.

4. A righthand-hitting outfielder with fine minor league numbers, this youngster is expected to be a formidable White Soxer of the future. While playing for the Cardinals' Louisville farm team he was the American Association's MVP in 1987.

5. The American League's Rookie of the Year in 1985, this fine-fielding shortstop made the All Star team in 1988. Originally property of the Padres, he was dealt to Chicago in December, 1984.

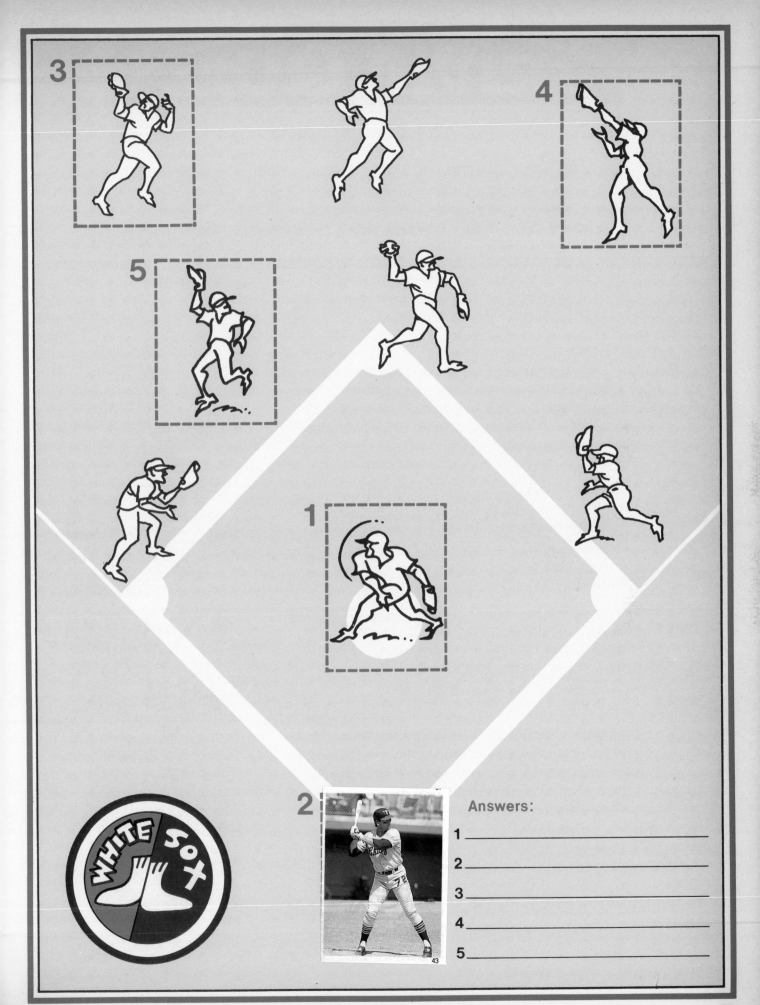

3

4

5

1

2

Answers:

1 _____

2 _____

3 _____

4 _____

5 _____

TRIVIA QUIZ

KANSAS CITY
ROYALS

Answers on page 94

Place stickers on opposite page

1. Another future Hall of Fame candidate, this lefthanded career .300 hitter plays first and third bases. Named to the American League All Star team for 13 straight seasons, he has hit 10 homers in postseason play for the Royals.

2. The sophomore jinx didn't hurt this righthanded-hitting third baseman in 1987. In fact he has hit .300 in his first three seasons with Kansas City. He had a six-hit game in August 1987, a year in which his 207 hits tied for the league lead.

3. This fine-throwing outfielder moved from the Mariners to the Royals in 1987 and celebrated the event by hitting 34 homers and knocking in 101 runs. His father, Jose, played in the American League in the 1960s and 1970s.

4. Now with his third AL club, this smooth-throwing southpaw previously pitched for Seattle and Chicago. In 1979, with the Mariners, he led the league with 209 strikeouts. He won 16 games for the Sox in 1983 and again in 1987.

5. A performer in both the American League and the National Football League, this righthanded slugger has gained great popularity in Kansas City. Though prone to striking out too much, he nevertheless hammers a baseball a long way. He also won the Heisman Award as a college football star in 1985.

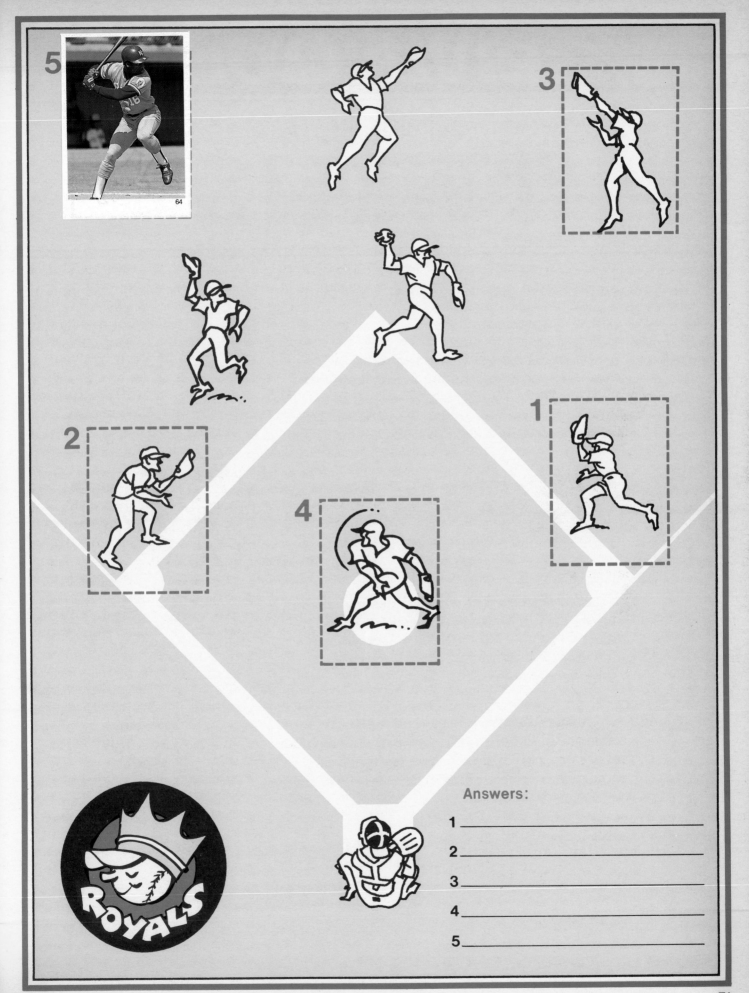

Answers:

1 _____

2 _____

3 _____

4 _____

5 _____

TRIVIA QUIZ

MINNESOTA
TWINS

Answers on page 94
Place stickers on opposite page

1. Obtained from the Giants before the 1987 season, this righthand-hitting outfielder is also a valuable basestealer. Though not rated a home-run hitter, he hit a grand-slam in the opener of the 1987 World Series.

2. A hometown product, this lefty slugger is among the Twins' home-run leaders ever year. In addition, he provides the ballclub with more than adequate defense around the first-base bag.

3. The 1987 World Series made him a nationally known pitching star and last season he continued among the game's top hurlers. He has pitched more than 200 innings in each of the past six seasons.

4. One of those who homered on his first major league at bat, in 1981, this righty-swinging infielder has been a contributing factor to the Twins ever since. He has been a prominent run producer the past three years.

5. His acquisition for the 1987 season gave Minnesota's bullpen the quality and stability it needed. A longtime relief star for Montreal, this hard-throwing righthander has well over 200 major league saves.

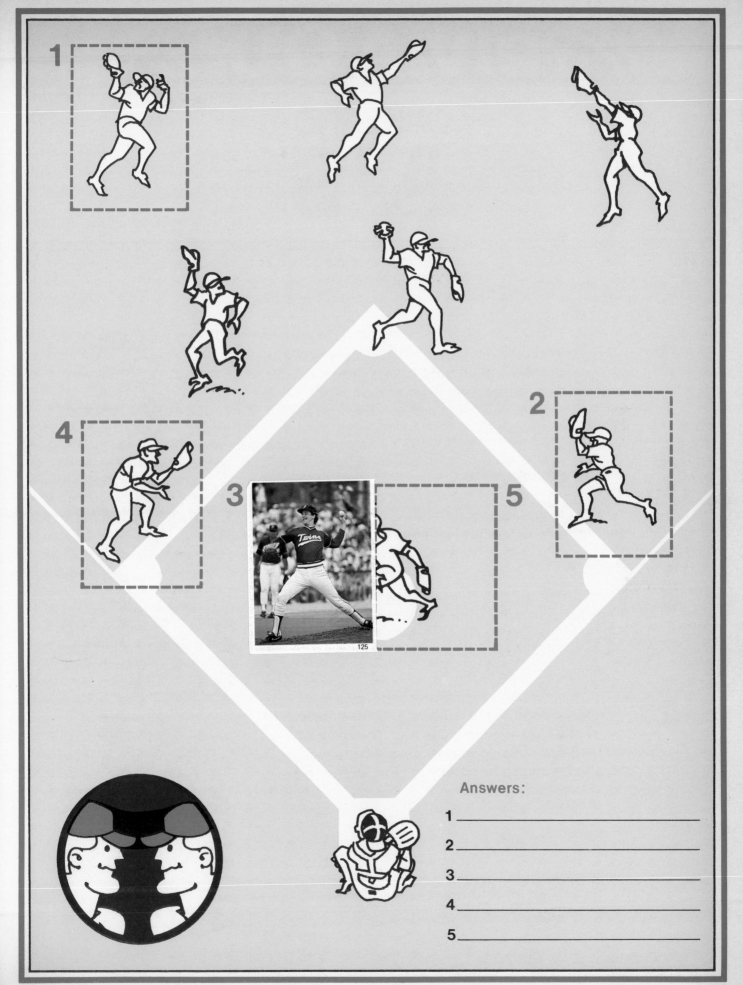

1 _____

2 _____

3 125

4 _____

5 _____

Answers:

1 _____

2 _____

3 _____

4 _____

5 _____

73

TRIVIA QUIZ

OAKLAND
A'S

Answers on page 94
Place stickers on opposite page

1. A .300 hitter five times in his 11-year American League career, this righthand-hitting third baseman was the AL's batting champion for Boston in 1981. He also provides sufficient defense, leading the AL third basemen in 1987.

2. His 49 home runs set a first-year record in 1987. That alone made him the AL's Rookie of the Year. A former Olympian from USC, he has made the All Star team in each of his first two seasons.

3. The Cuban-born slugger is not only a future home-run champion, but his ability to steal bases enhances his value to the A's. Along with the quantity of his four-base hits is the distance he achieves on many of them.

4. This veteran righthander, a 20-game winner for Boston in 1978, switched to the bullpen the past two years in Oakland and seemingly has found a brand new career. In 1988 he led the AL in saves.

5. This righthander pitched for the Dodgers, Rangers and Phillies with no marked success before arriving in Oakland as a 20-game winner in 1987. Prior to that he'd never won more than nine games in any season.

Answers:

1 _____

2 _____

3 _____

4 _____

5 _____

SEATTLE
MARINERS

Answers on page 94
Place stickers on opposite page

1. This lefthander, one of the AL's premier strikeout artists, led the league in Ks in 1986 and 1987. He won 17 games as a rookie in 1984, the most by a freshman southpaw since 1963 when Gary Peters won 19 for the White Sox.

2. After pitching the 1985 and 1986 seasons with the Mariners, this righthander was sidelined in 1987 by an elbow operation. A member of the 1984 Olympic squad, he was Seattle's No. 1 draft pick that year and advanced to the majors after only 39 innings of minor league ball.

3. He spent seven seasons in the minors before joining the Mariners in 1984. A high school baseball star in his native New York City, this righthanded hitter, though often hampered by injuries, continues to improve.

4. This lefthand-hitting first baseman, the American League's Rookie of the Year in 1984, is annually among the Mariners' most productive performers. Another of the Arizona State University players to make the majors, he was Seattle's All Star game representative in his first year.

5. His 60 stolen bases were tops in the American League in 1987 and for each of the last two years he has made the AL All Star team. Not a powerhitter, his defensive work around second is widely recognized and greatly appreciated.

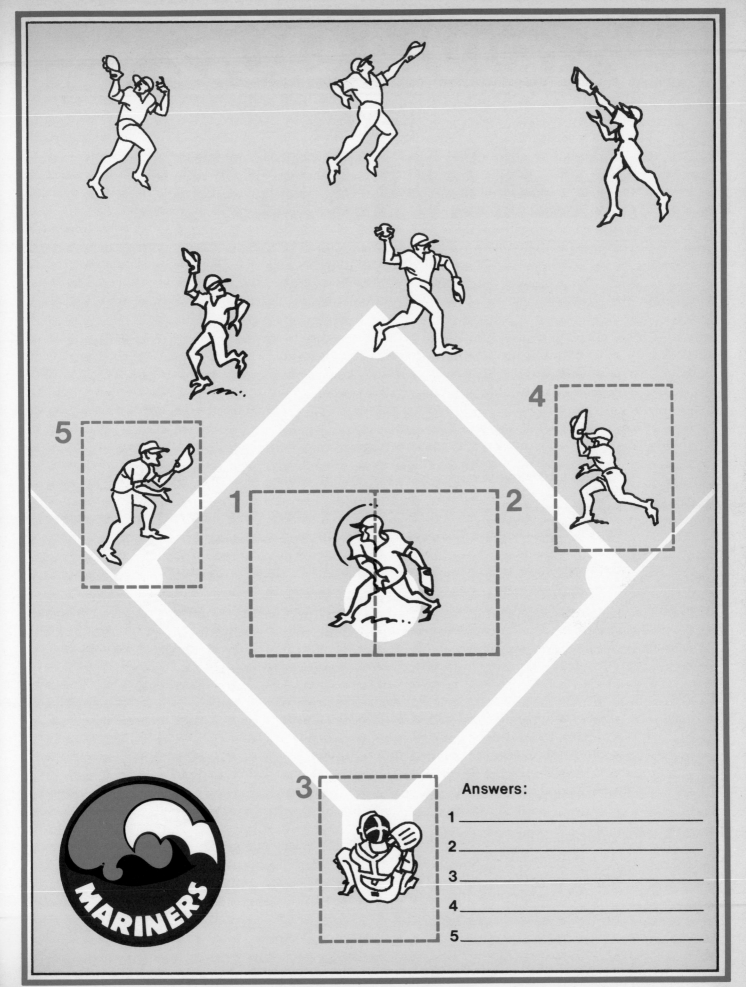

Answers:

1 _____

2 _____

3 _____

4 _____

5 _____

TRIVIA QUIZ

TEXAS
RANGERS

Answers on page 94
Place stickers on opposite page

1. A lefthand-hitting longballer, this first baseman has given the Rangers consistency both at the plate and in the field for the past half dozen seasons.

2. This righthanded-hitting product of Oklahoma State University is a hit-and-miss situation. Although a big home-run hitter, he also is among the American League's strikeout leaders each year.

3. This ex-Dodger is a knuckleball hurler with 20 years in the majors. He has pitched the past nine seasons for the Rangers and consistently wins in double figures for them.

4. Traded from the White Sox in December 1985, this righty won a dozen games for the Rangers in his first season. His 1987 season ended in July because of shoulder problems and subsequent surgery idled him much of last year.

5. A switchhitting outfielder whose defensive ability is causing rival baserunners some concern, this fellow has power at the plate. He hit 30 homers in 1987 and became the first major leaguer in 22 years to hit that many at the age of 21.

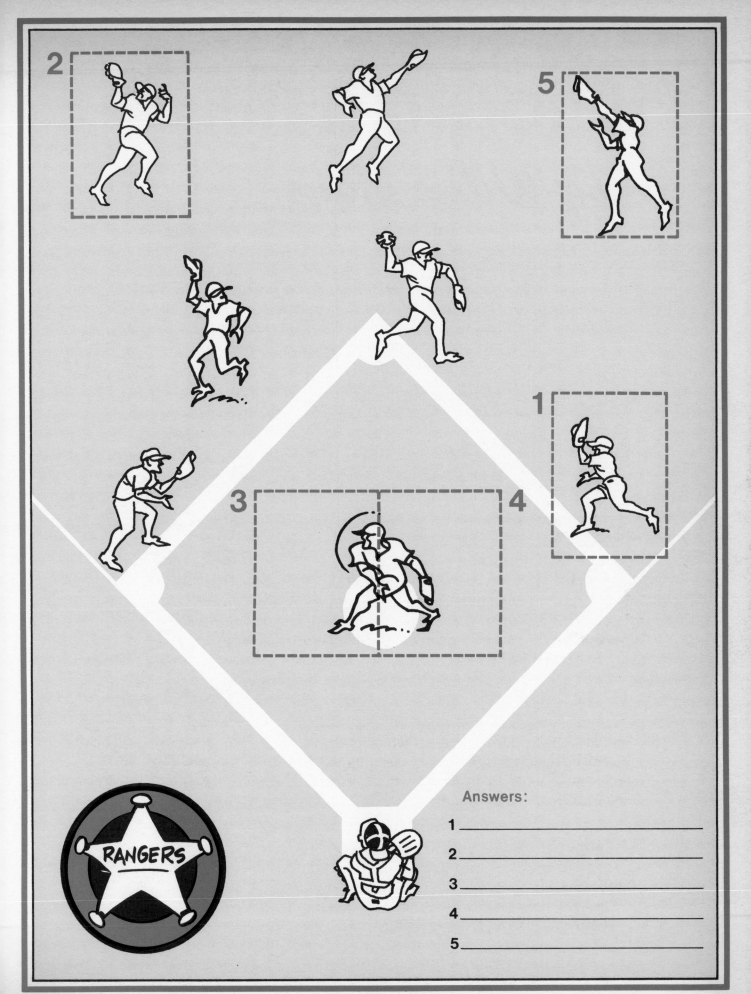

Answers:

1 _____

2 _____

3 _____

4 _____

5 _____

FIELDING TIPS
by Willie Mays

Defense makes up more than 50% of the game. In order to win, you not only have to know how to score runs, but also how to stop the opposition. The great outfielder Willie Mays was inducted into the Hall of Fame in August 1979. He is considered one of the most complete ballplayers who ever played the game. On the field, he did just about everything that could be done. I've asked Willie to share with you a few basic tips about playing good defense.

1 To be a good fielders, you must be aggressive. You must go after every hit ball with everything you have. Don't let the ball go after you.

2 A good fielder is also a thinking fielder. He knows what he's going to do with the ball even before it's hit. When he catches the ball, he knows where to make the throw to prevent or save runs.

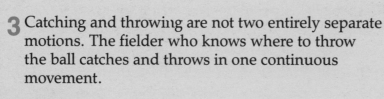

3 Catching and throwing are not two entirely separate motions. The fielder who knows where to throw the ball catches and throws in one continuous movement.

4 Never be afraid of the ball. If you keep the ball in front of you and your eye on it at all times, there is little chance that you will be hurt by a batted ball.

5 In the field, get yourself into a comfortable position where you feel flexible and can move quickly. Most players do this by standing on the balls of their feet, feet apart, knees flexed, the upper part of their bodies bent slightly forward and with the arms relaxed in front of them.

6 The glove is only a tool to help you catch the ball. Before using a glove, practice catching barehanded with a tennis ball. When catching, develop "soft" hands, which means your hands move with the ball into your body. Catch the ball with two hands. When the ball falls into the pocket of the glove, squeeze the gloved hand softly.

7 In catching a fly ball, don't let your eyes leave the ball until the moment it's squeezed in your glove. In playing the outfield, learn to judge the height, speed, direction and distance of the ball in order to be in a position to catch it.

8 A good fielder needs a strong and accurate arm. Practice throwing to home plate and all the bases from the outfield ten to fifteen minutes every day. This will help you stretch muscles and improve both strength and accuracy.

9 Grip the ball across the seams and throw overhand. Throwing overhand gives the ball straighter and better carry. To get "zip" on the ball, make sure your feet are planted firmly on the ground when you make the catch.

10 Don't be afraid to learn how to field more than one position. A versatile player is often a big asset to his team.

YOU MAKE THE CALL

How many bases are awarded a runner when, on a pickoff try, the pitcher throws wild and the ball goes into the stands?

Answer: When a pitcher, from the rubber, throws into a dugout or the stands, each runner is entitled to advance one base.

Is it a home run when a fielder goes to the outfield fence near the foul pole and jumps, only to have the ball bounce off his glove and into the stands?

Answer: It's a homer if the deflected ball goes over the fence in fair territory. But if the deflected ball lands on the foul side of the pole it's a two-base hit.

Is a baserunner out if, as he approaches home plate, he's accidently hit by a thrown ball and falls down, only to be tagged by a fielder?

Answer: Yes, an injury such as this one may be regrettable, but the runner, when legally tagged, is out.

Is it a legal out if, with the bases loaded and two out, a batter fans and the catcher muffs the pitch but recovers the ball and tags the plate?

Answer: Yes, it's the third out because on the misplay the batter is entitled to run to first and the other runners are forced to advance.

What happens to the baserunner when he attempts to steal second and the batter, after swinging and missing, but not stepping across home plate, interferes with the catcher's throw?

Answer: The batter is out for interference and the runner is returned to first base.

Is it a fair ball when a batted ball bounces off the third-base bag and hits the runner leading off that base in foul ground?

Answer: It's a fair ball and remains in play because it hit the base, which is in fair ground, before striking the runner who was in foul territory.

TEAM NAME
WORD SEARCH

Answer on page 95

Hidden in the letters on the opposite page are the names of all 26 Major League teams. They may appear either forward or backward, up and down, across or diagonally. Circle each one as you find it and write the name below.

To get you started, the first name is circled for you.

1 Yonkees
2 Mets
3 Cubs
4 Braves
5 Red Sox
6 ~~Tigers~~ Tigers
7 Astros
8 white Sox
9 ORIOLES
10 Mariners
11 Giants
12 Dodgers
13 Angels

14 Royals
15 Padres
16 A's
17 Rangers
18 Phillies
19 Blue jays
20 Reds
21 indians
22 Expos
23 Cardinals
24 Twins
25 Brewers
26 Pirates

G	A	D	R	E	'	S	Y	A	B	M	A	O
I	R	O	Y	A	L	S	R	E	V	R	A	
A	I	D	A	S	T	E	T	W	I	N	S	
N	P	G	U	T	W	S	P	H	G	I	T	
T	O	E	S	E	I	L	L	I	H	P		
S	X	R	R	N	E	X	P	T	L	I	O	
O	G	S	D	P	A	D	R	E	S	R	S	
S	B	L	U	E	J	A	Y	S	K	A	O	
R	A	H	W	I	E	A	L	O	E	T	M	
E	N	T	H	V	N	A	S	X	E	E	S	
N	G	I	A	K	N	D	P	B	S	S	E	
I	E	G	E	I	G	O	I	R	R	D	L	
R	L	E	D	X	S	V	O	A	G	E	O	
A	S	R	O	B	A	Y	R	V	N	R	I	
M	A	S	U	R	A	N	G	E	R	S	R	
C	U	C	B	E	R	E	D	S	O	X	O	

END OF YEAR

WINNERS, LEADERS & CHAMPIONS

How many end-of-the-year leaders and winners can you pick? You won't have all the answers until after the end of the season in October.

A90 DIVISION WINNERS *1991*

Red Sox
American League East Team

Athletics
American League West Team

Pirates
National League East Team

Reds
National League West Team

DIVISION CHAMPS

1990 PENNANT WINNERS *1991*

Athletics
American League Team

Reds
National League Team

AL NL

1990 WORLD SERIES WINNER *1991*

Reds
Team

NUMBER 1

BATTING AVERAGE CHAMPIONS

_____

American League Player

_____

National League Player

HOME-RUN CHAMPIONS

_____

American League Player

_____

National League Player

RBI CHAMPIONS

_____

American League Players

_____

National League Players

STOLEN-BASE CHAMPIONS

_____

American League Player

_____

National League Player

MOST VICTORIES BY A PITCHER

_____

American League Player

_____

National League Player

STRIKEOUT LEADERS

American League Player
_____

National League Player

E.R.A. LEADERS

American League Player
_____

National League Player

MOST VALUABLE PLAYER AWARDS

American League Player
_____

National League Player

CY YOUNG AWARDS

American League Player
_____

National League Player

FINAL TEAM STANDINGS

AMERICAN LEAGUE EAST

1 _____

2 _____

3 _____

4 _____

5 _____

6 _____

7 _____

NATIONAL LEAGUE EAST

1 _____

2 _____

3 _____

4 _____

5 _____

6 _____

AMERICAN LEAGUE WEST

1 _____

2 _____

3 _____

4 _____

5 _____

6 _____

7 _____

NATIONAL LEAGUE WEST

1 _____

2 _____

3 _____

4 _____

5 _____

6 _____

THE 1952 TOPPS BASEBALL CARDS

This is the first standard size series of cards produced by the famous TOPPS Company. There were 407 cards included in the series. It is the most sought after baseball card series manufactured after World War II. The series includes the first Topps card of Mickey Mantle which is presently valued at $6,500.00 in mint condition. Due to its scarcity, the complete set lists at $36,000.00 in mint condition. The following is a listing of the highest valued cards in the series: (Values pertain to mint condition).

Cards Courtesy of The Topps Co.

MICKEY MANTLE
CARD #311 $6500

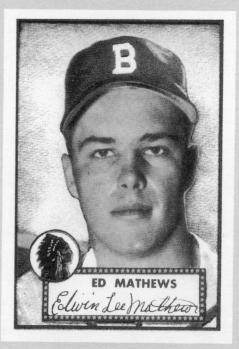

ED MATHEWS
CARD #407 $1600

ROY CAMPANELLA
CARD #314 $1200

WILLIE MAYS
CARD #261 $875

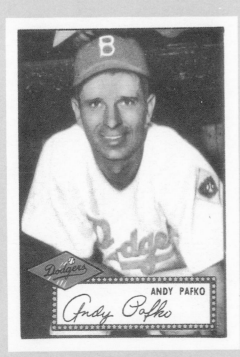

ANDY PAFKO
CARD #1 $850

JACKIE ROBINSON
CARD #312 $725

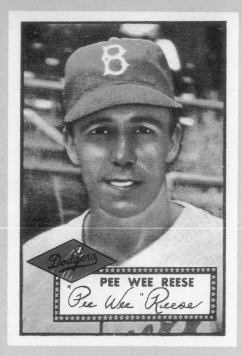

PEE WEE REESE
CARD #333 $500

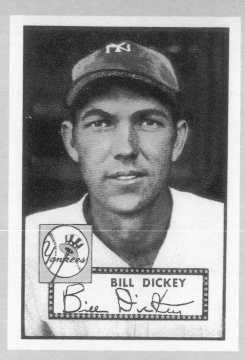

BILL DICKEY
CARD #400 $500

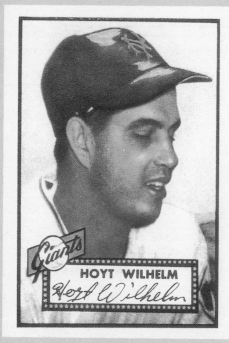

HOYT WILHELM
CARD #392 $400

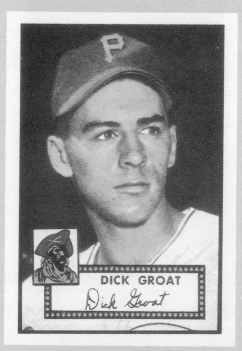

DICK GROAT
CARD #369 $250

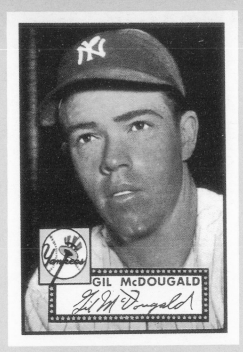

GIL McDOUGALD

CARD #372 $250

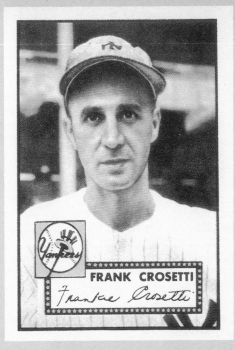

FRANK CROSETTI

CARD #384 $250

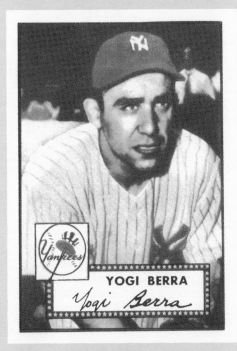

YOGI BERRA

CARD #191 $225

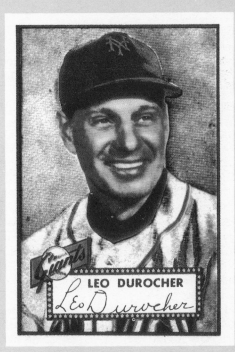

LEO DUROCHER

CARD #315 $225

ANSWERS TO TRIVIA QUIZ

CHICAGO CUBS
1. Rafael Palmeiro
2. Andre Dawson
3. Greg Maddux
4. Jody Davis
5. Shawon Dunston

MONTREAL EXPOS
1. Andres Galarraga
2. Tim Raines
3. Tim Wallach
4. Tim Burke
5. Hubie Brooks

NEW YORK METS
1. Dwight Gooden
2. Keith Hernandez
3. David Cone
4. Gary Carter
5. Darryl Strawberry

PHILADELPHIA PHILLIES
1. Mike Schmidt
2. Juan Samuel
3. Milt Thompson
4. Von Hayes
5. Chris James

PITTSBURGH PIRATES
1. Bobby Bonilla
2. Mike Lavalliere
3. Brian Fisher
4. Jose Lind
5. Barry Bonds

ST. LOUIS CARDINALS
1. Mike Brunansky
2. Ozzie Smith
3. Luis Alicea
4. John Tudor
5. Jose Deleon

ATLANTA BRAVES
1. Dale Murphy
2. Zane Smith
3. Bruce Sutter
4. Ozzie Virgil
5. Gerald Perry

CINCINNATI REDS
1. John Franco
2. Barry Larkin
3. Bo Diaz
4. Kal Daniels
5. Eric Davis

HOUSTON ASTROS
1. Nolan Ryan
2. Mike Scott
3. Glenn Davis
4. Bill Doran
5. Alan Ashby

LOS ANGELES DODGERS
1. Pedro Guerrero
2. Kirk Gibson
3. Steve Sax
4. Orel Hershiser
5. Fernando Valenzuela

SAN DIEGO PADRES
1. John Kruk
2. Tony Gwynn
3. Benito Santiago
4. Roberto Alomar
5. Mark Davis

SAN FRANCISCO GIANTS
1. Rob Thompson
2. Candy Maldonado
3. Will Clark
4. Mike LaCoss
5. Scott Garrelts

BALTIMORE ORIOLES
1. Cal Ripken, Jr.
2. Eddie Murray
3. Fred Lynn
4. Billy Ripken
5. Rick Schu

BOSTON RED SOX
1. Roger Clemens
2. Lee Smith
3. Dwight Evans
4. Wade Boggs
5. Jody Reed

CLEVELAND INDIANS
1. Joe Carter
2. Brook Jacoby
3. Greg Swindell
4. Tom Candiotti
5. Mel Hall

DETROIT TIGERS
1. Matt Nokes
2. Alan Trammell
3. Doyle Alexander
4. Jack Morris
5. Frank Tanana

MILWAUKEE BREWERS
1. Paul Molitor
2. Robin Yount
3. Rob Deer
4. Ted Higuera
5. Chris Bosio

NEW YORK YANKEES
1. Dave Winfield
2. Dave Righetti
3. Jack Clark
4. Willie Randolph
5. Don Mattingly

TORONTO BLUE JAYS
1. Tony Fernandez
2. George Bell
3. Mike Flanagan
4. Lloyd Moseby
5. Jesse Barfield

CALIFORNIA ANGELS
1. Wally Joyner
2. Mike Witt
3. Johnny Ray
4. Chili Davis
5. Jack Howell

CHICAGO WHITE SOX
1. Melido Perez
2. Carlton Fisk
3. Ivan Calderon
4. Lance Johnson
5. Ozzie Guillen

KANSAS CITY ROYALS
1. George Brett
2. Kevin Seitzer
3. Danny Tartabull
4. Floyd Bannister
5. Bo Jackson

MINNESOTA TWINS
1. Dan Gladden
2. Kent Hrbek
3. Frank Viola
4. Gary Gaetti
5. Jeff Reardon

OAKLAND ATHLETICS
1. Carney Lansford
2. Mark McGwire
3. Jose Canseco
4. Dennis Eckersley
5. Dave Stewart

SEATTLE MARINERS
1. Mark Langston
2. Bill Swift
3. Dave Valle
4. Alvin Davis
5. Harold Reynolds

TEXAS RANGERS
1. Pete O'Brien
2. Pete Incaviglia
3. Charlie Hough
4. Ed Correa
5. Ruben Sierra

ANSWER TO TEN HALL OF FAMERS — WHO AM I?

1. Hank Aaron
2. Mickey Mantle
3. Willie Mays
4. Ted Williams
5. Babe Ruth
6. Ty Cobb
7. Honus Wagner
8. Cy Young
9. Christy Mathewson
10. Joe DiMaggio

ANSWER TO TEAM NAME WORD SEARCH

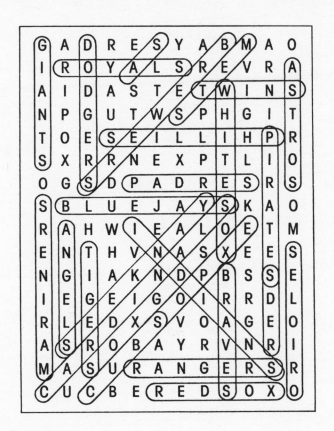

BASEBALL CAMPS

One of the best ways to improve your baseball skills is to attend baseball "school" or camp for a vacation. You can write for brochures from the listings below:

DOYLE BASEBALL SCHOOL
P.O. Box 9156
Winter Haven, Florida 33883

PHIL WILSON'S SHO-ME BASEBALL CAMP
Star Route 4 Box 198-A
Reeds Spring, Missouri 65737

MICKEY OWEN BASEBALL SCHOOL
Miller, Missouri 65707

TOM BELCHER BASEBALL CAMP
Box 395
Chandler, Oklahoma 74834

HALL OF FAME SPORTS ACADEMY (baseball brochure)
2546 Cropsey Ave.
Brooklyn, N.Y. 11214

'PLAY BALL' BASEBALL ACADEMY
P.O. Box S
Buzzards Bay, Massachusetts 02532